To: E

MW00534182

HERE NOW ONE

A Practical Guide to
the Spiritual Life

*May this be a resource to you
on your own ever unfolding
spiritual journey*

Terry Moore *With warmest wishes,*

Terry
2021

New Sarum Press
United Kingdom

HERE NOW ONE
First published by New Sarum Press January 2021
Copyright ©2021 Terry Moore
Copyright ©2021 New Sarum Press

ISBN: 978-1-8383836-0-2

NEW SARUM PRESS
www.newsarumpress.com

Table of Contents

Foreword by Greg Goode

THIS BOOK IS A COLLECTION OF ESSAYS AND spiritual advice from a Sufi master. The writings reveal Sufism to be a viable, active spiritual path with a nondual heart. I'll say more about the nondual connection below, but first I'd like to talk about the author, who is a good friend of mine. Terry Moore was raised in the American Midwest and for over forty years he has also been known by the Islamic name Sidi Al-Bashir, "bringer of good news."

The Author

Terry defines Sufism as "Islamic mysticism," and his journey took him through several notable stops along the way. From Pyotr Ouspenskii and George Gurdjieff, he was inspired by the import of mystical inner work. From Mircea Eliade and other twentieth-century proponents of the Perennial Philosophy (see the reading list at the end), Terry came to appreciate the importance of tradition as giving shape to one's inner work.

The Perennialists' approach to mysticism combines these two important insights:

> Firstly, there exists a divine reality that the various religions express in different ways.

> Secondly, knowing this, we should practice one and only one of these religions.

These two insights bring together knowledge and wisdom. They allow a vast theoretical perspective to become grounded with a concrete spiritual approach to the divine.

Of these approaches, Terry was drawn to Sufism. He has often told me that the Perennialists tended to regard Advaita Vedanta as the gold standard for the clear articulation of non-dual wisdom, yet most of them actually joined mystical Sufi orders rather than espousing Hinduism. Terry followed suit. By the time he encountered Sufism, there was a secret Sufi order or *tariqah* in the United States. This was the order that he joined, and over the decades he rose to increasingly important positions of leadership and mentorship. He finds the Sufi teachings to be true to both nondual insight and the Perennial Philosophy.

Terry and I met several years ago, when he was also a student of the Direct Path. He explained to me that the Sufi teachings he inherited were exceedingly rich in vision and doctrine, but that he would like to do more to make the vision a living experience for himself and his students. The Direct Path was able to help. He actually discusses this point in the final essay, "On Religion and the Direct Path", which he originally wrote for the 2019 anthology I edited for New Sarum Press, called *Real-World Nonduality: Reports from the Field.*

The Book

Back to Terry's book. The material here originated as various forms of spiritual writings composed from 2006 to 2020. These writings consist of spiritual advice, encouragement, and education. They include letters, emails, guidance in a question and answer format, essays, spiritual discourses, and sermons. Sometimes the audience consisted of groups, sometimes individuals. With the exception of "On Religion and the Direct Path", which originally had a nondual audience, the context was almost always his Sufi *tariqah*.

The writings are organized by topic. Topics include the meaning of existence, God as our guide, the spiritual path, prayer, sacred texts, practice and effort, living in the world, self-transformation, emotions, and virtues and vices. The unifying purpose is always to provide guidance to students on how best to assimilate the teachings of the *tariqah* into their daily lives.

Sufis and non-Sufis can enjoy the book. Terry writes in a remarkably humble, non-technical, down-to-earth style. Here are a few randomly selected quotes that may whet your appetite while also expressing the Sufi flavor of Terry's approach:

"Question: *Do you believe in the Divine Unity?"*

"Response: The answer to that question is, first of all, yes, I do. That's one of our first principles."

"We must approach a sacred text on its terms, not on ours."

"God isn't interested in what we know; He is interested in who we are."

"The very purpose of creation is to lead you to God. The path to Him is not away from the world, but through it."

Traditions and Nonduality

Recalling some of the topics covered in the book, I'd like to address a question that might be asked by readers more familiar with non-traditional nonduality than with Sufism:

"But what do practice and effort, virtues and vices, and sacred texts have to do with nondual realization?"

The answer is "A lot!" Not every spiritual communication, in order to be helpful, needs to end in a magnificent nondual flourish that equates the reader with global awareness. Sometimes people have smaller or more practical questions. Sometimes the questions and concerns are rooted in a specific tradition. Terry answers these questions in a kindly and prescient way, meeting the questioners where they present themselves, and gently pointing them upwards. I find that all the topics in his book are relevant to the grounding necessary to foster a more global, unitive lived experience.

Major traditions tend to agree on the importance of preparatory ground. For example, the Vedantic path divides spiritual practices into different *yogas* or ways of unifying with the Absolute. The yogas can be thought of as types of activity that apply to a wide variety of spiritual traditions, not just to Hinduism or Vedanta. A basic list of the yogas includes *karma yoga* (the path of selfless service), *bhakti yoga* (the path of devotion), *raja yoga* (self-inquiry or the path of disciplining the body and mind), and *jnana yoga* (the path of inquiry into the real vs. the unreal). I find that these types of activities can be found in Sufism, Vedanta, and all the other major religious traditions I'm familiar with. They also apply to even the most stripped-down, non-traditional types of nonduality teaching.

There is a time-tested wisdom behind this breakdown of categories. The yogas work together in different balances for different people, and each yoga utilizes different personal, physical, and psychological factors to lead us to nondual realization. Think of the various practices prescribed by traditional religions, such as reading traditional texts and performing service, prayers, meditations, recitations, and inquiries. They all work by leveraging different aspects of the human person. Different people respond to different types and combinations of these yogas. To paraphrase a Zen adage, if spiritual realization is a divine accident, these activities make one accident-prone.

One of my own Vedanta teachers emphasized the importance of *jnana yoga* self-inquiry for nondual realization. But he quickly added, "You can't do inquiry if your mind doesn't stay on topic. So you may need *raja yoga*. But you can't discipline your mind if your emotions are unstable. So you may need *bhakti yoga*. And you can't do devotion if your body is sore and fidgety. So you may need *karma yoga*." Each of the yogas participates in our path by making an integrated, living nondual realization easier to attain.

When we look at a traditional nondual path in this way, we see the relevance of the topics and small questions covered in Terry's book. Each topic aligns with one of the various yogas. Nothing is irrelevant. I know Terry to be a man of God and a man of wisdom, and I hope you will like the book as much as I do!

Acknowledgments

To ALL THE INDIVIDUALS I HAVE HAD THE opportunity to share my life with and learn from, I want to say thank you for making this book a reality.

Without the experiences of and support from my wife, friends, and mentors, this book would not exist. Thank you to my loving wife, Lynn, to my dear friend Larry, who has always served as an extra lobe of my brain, and to Berta, who has shared so much of my journey.

In addition, I would like to thank my spiritual teachers—too many to mention here—for all their wonderful lessons and insights. The principals in this large group would be Frithjof Schuon, Martin Lings, Seyyed Hossein Nasr, James Cutsinger, Greg Goode, and Francis Lucille.

Having an idea and turning it into a book is as hard as it sounds. The experience is both internally challenging and rewarding. I especially want to thank the individuals who helped make this happen. Complete thanks to Abigail Tardiff, Anjali Kapil, and Farasha Euker.

Preface

A LONG TIME AGO, OR SO IT SEEMS TO ME NOW, I became convinced that there is a final truth to existence and a final reality that includes all other apparent realities. Over a period of years, I explored the available information in search of a philosophy, a teaching, or a teacher to open this question for me and help me find an answer.

By a long and circuitous route, I found the world of classical mysticism, most of which is instantiated in religious traditions. This was quite a surprise, and I once remarked, "How clever of God to have hidden the truth in religion—who would think to look for it there?" But that is where I found it, and that is essentially the background of my exposition. This is not to say I believe that the truth is limited to religious expression, for—I say this as a religious person—that would limit God.

In any event, my own path brought me into religion—in my case, Islam and the practice of its mysticism, known as Sufism.

Having acquired familiarity with the practice and, what is vastly more important, my own experience of the practice, I have often been called upon to teach, advise, and guide others on the "path to enlightenment."

This book is drawn from a collection of my essays, letters, and presentations over these years, and these excerpts are presented here in the hope that the questions, answers, and formulations they contain may be of value to other seekers of truth and travelers on the path. I say "the path" with the understanding that there is not simply one path to truth, but many paths up the mountain, or, as is said in Islam, "There are as many paths to Allah as there are sons of Adam." Clearly, as Orson Welles said, "we are born alone, we die alone," and every man and woman must find and negotiate this landscape himself or herself.

My orientation here is Universalist[1] and Perennialist.[2] Although much of the context of what I write is situated within the Islamic and Sufi metaphor, I believe these principles and directions for the understanding and operation of the interior spiritual life are also universal and perennial.

This book is about the practical application of spiritual techniques to enrich our life and practice. This book is not about doctrine or philosophy. It does not tout a particular religion. The perspective presented here is completely uninterested in religious polemics and in questions about who or what is better or righter. I have tried to maintain this determined non-judgmentalism throughout the book, as I do in life. My only interest here is in being of principial or practical help to my fellow travelers as we journey from our illusion of separativity to the reality of the One.

---

1. Universalism here means the belief in what Fritjof Schuon calls "the transcendent unity of religions."
2. A Perennialist is someone who believes in the Perennial Philosophy, a perspective in spirituality that views all of the world's religious traditions as sharing a single, metaphysical truth or origin from which all esoteric and exoteric knowledge and doctrine has grown.

Introduction—To God through the World: An Existential and Practical Metaphysics

THIS IS WRITTEN FOR YOU IF YOU KNOW THAT the purpose of your life is to seek God, but you find that the world around you constantly gets in your way. Do you believe that the best way to move toward God is, therefore, to separate yourself from the world as much as you can? I am here to tell you that the opposite is true. The very purpose of creation is to lead you to God. The path to Him is not away from the world, but through it.

It's not hard to understand why we are convinced that we can only find God if we hold the world at arm's length. The good things in the world distract us from God when we desire them instead of Him. The evil things distract us by causing us, in our suffering, to turn our attention to ourselves instead of to Him. The experiences of the body distract us from the life of the mind, and the machinations of our minds distract us from the knowledge of the heart. We find ourselves, as Housman put it, "a stranger and afraid / In a world I never made."[3]

Besides these normal human struggles in learning how to live in the world, we face another confusion. We are believers, so we reject the modern suggestion that life is meaningless. But in the last little epoch of human history, the scientific method has come to dominate our thinking. To be sure, science has given us many insights into the workings of the cosmos. It has provided us with marvelous powers over nature. But when we

---

3. *The Laws of God, the Laws of Man* by A.E.Housman.
www.housman-society.co.uk [online accessed 23 December 2020]

invite the voice of science to join the voice of faith in explain-
ing to us who and what we are, the picture we end up with is
a baffling amalgam of disharmonious parts. We have come to
believe, explicitly or implicitly, that we are—somehow—a spark
of intelligence that lives in a colloidal mass of cells imprisoned
in a bony skull and bag of flesh, and that we are surrounded by a
world of titanic forces, unthinking and mechanical, that control
our destiny. No wonder we don't know how to live.

Today's educated person respects the scientific method and
the validity of the insights it offers. We know that there is no
need to choose between science and God—but there isn't certainty about what the two have to do with each other. So we
end up living in two separate realms: the realm of meaning,
spirituality, religion, faith, and God on the one hand; and the
realm of random, meaningless, cold and dead matter on the
other. The modern human doesn't know how to integrate these
two realms, and in fact doesn't even realize that that these
realms should be integrated.

We must cast off this tacit cosmology whose spell we have
been living under. We must reject the assumption that being
consists of two realms with no commerce between them: the
realm of spiritual meaning and the realm of empty fact. In its
place, I offer you an *existential metaphysics*: an understanding
of the purpose of creation *for you*. I offer you an account of the
reason for the world and our place in it that is opposed neither
to modern scientific knowledge nor to our inner conviction that
the world has meaning, and that human life has purpose. And I
offer practical advice based on this understanding of the created
world, designed specifically for the thinking person, on how to
live immersed in the world so that it fulfills its purpose, which
is to lead you to God.

Chapter 1

On Religion and Faith

RELIGION TELLS US OUR POSITION IN THE universe and tries to draw conclusions about what that means. It's also a means of getting closer to the good, to God, and to being in harmony with it. Faith comes from having seen some of it. It's funny, you know: in the Bible it says, "Blessed are those who have not seen and have believed." (John 20:29) But you have to see some before you can have faith about what you can't see.

Faith is more than belief. Faith means that you have some experiential evidence and that there's an active component in keeping that channel open: not simply believing it and putting it on the shelf, but believing it and keeping it open, operatively, with renewal and practice. That renewal and practice is instantiated in religion. Religion—real religion—is not an intellectual activity; it involves all the dimensions of our being. Religion seeks to transform and integrate all of our parts and make us whole. The word *holy* at root means *whole*. Religion seeks to make us holy.

Religion, after all, has as its purpose the integration of the entire being into a Divine harmony. Consequently, every authentic tradition speaks to the whole human person, to the spirit and the soul and the body, and by bringing all of these levels of the microcosm into play—by providing doctrine for the mind, moral precepts for the will, objects of devotion for the sentiment, and ritual for the body—tradition serves to protect us against the hypertrophy or deviation of any one of these levels.

There are many religions to choose from, but we must choose one. Only one. This is not to say that we can't appreciate and draw wisdom from them all, but we can't practice them all. As they say in Zen: "It is better to dig a well a hundred feet deep than to dig ten wells that are each ten feet deep."

3

I am a Muslim. This was a choice I made (Was it? Or was it made for me?) at the end of a long search for answers to fundamental questions. What I was looking for was a teacher/guide/master who knew and who could help me know. I didn't know much about Islam, and I had never been very interested in it. But I was open to whatever came my way. I explored lots of things (including many dark alleys). Eventually, by the grace of God, I found Perennialism. This was, finally, the lens through which I could see the truth.

Unfortunately, though, we can't practice Perennialism, as it has no form. It is a smile without a cat. It is an intellectual perspective. In order to be operative, it must be packaged in a form that allows practice. The package it comes in is orthodox religion. This is not to say that the way to enlightenment is closed elsewhere, for "the Spirit blows where it listeth." (John 3:8) It is just that there are more risks and uncertainties outside of the major revelations and their scriptures. Certainly "With God all things are possible," (Matthew 9:26) yet, as I learned from the Perennialists, He reveals religion so that He may "re-bind" us to Him. This is the very definition of "religion."

So the question for me became: *Is there a teacher within a formal religion?* I found the teaching and the teachers I was looking for in Perennialism. The Perennialists I knew were mostly Muslims. Their spiritual master was a Muslim. So I entered Islam.

Question: *Is the study of religion necessary for advancement on the path?*

Response: There is a tremendous tendency, once you have discovered the path, to want to throw yourself into the study of religion and philosophy. But this is a matter of taste and temperament. You can study it if you like. You can make a career there if you feel called to. But there is nothing about the actual working of the path that calls for academic study of any kind.

Further, you will find that the academic study of religion is not particularly conducive to the path. Religion as taught in universities tends to be a mixture of history, sociology, and psychology. You would almost certainly be disappointed with the focus of the instruction and the quality and motives of your colleagues. This is not a decision that should be based on your desire to transcend yourself on the path. This is a matter of making a logical career choice.

In any event, let your heart rest easy. The choice of a career is of secondary importance with respect to the path. Choosing to study religion may seems like a momentous decision—and from some standpoints it is—but whatever you choose, and wherever you end up, you will find the one-and-only element that constitutes the ground of the path: yourself. That is what the path is all about; it is about you. So long as you seek Him, your decision can't be wrong. In doing so, you will learn much about reality, religion, tradition, the world, good and evil, etc. In time, you will know a great deal. But God isn't interested in what we know; He is interested in who we are.

Question: *Do you believe in the Divine Unity?*

Response: The answer to that question is, first of all, yes, I do. That's one of our first principles. But as we look at the way we live our lives in the world around us, we often behave as if we don't. We see things separately. We look around ourselves and we see a world full of objects and people and experiences, and we see that they are different, and we tend to ascribe to them a reality that they really don't have. The part of us that does that, we often assume, is our own unity, from which we get to assess these differences.

Yet if we look at ourselves, what do we really find? We find that we are a collection of beliefs, a collection of experiences, a collection of feelings and facts, and it's really very disparate.

We know that there's this mélange of characteristics and attitudes and beliefs inside of ourselves. And some of them are certainly not real. We look at them and we try sometimes to watch them engage one another and to battle for dominance. A good idea versus a bad idea. A good characteristic versus a bad characteristic. And we try in our own way to foster the good and the right as best we can, and there's certainly a place for that.

That's the wrong battle. The battle on the path is discernment.[4] The question really isn't, *Which of these qualities are more or less good?* but, *Can we interrogate all of them to see if they're real or not?* Because that's the question: Is it real or is it part of the illusion? And if we explore and question and engage our own beliefs, we will find very often that they're not real, that they're false. They're part of the fantasy. And when that happens, when these attitudes and beliefs are exposed to the truth, they surrender to it.

But that surrender is not the kind of conquering that we find in most confrontations. It's not as if they vanish or they somehow magically disappear. What happens is that when we discover them to be false, we simply take them less seriously. And when we do that, they become less a part of our consciousness and awareness and our sphere of thought and action. And they play less and less of a role in our lives. This is really the meat of the path. This is why it's a path and not simply a system or a philosophy. Because that encounter, and that confrontation of discernment, is key to everything. And when the false notions and beliefs and ideas confront the real, they submit. But it's a submission of peace. It's not a submission of conquest; it's a Divine victory. It's the victory of peace, and it's the victory of the false submitting to the true, which is in the nature of things.

---

4. Discernment is the ability to see things for what they really are and not for what you want them to be.

Question: *If God is everywhere, then why do we not see God everywhere?*

Response: God is One. There is a Divine Unity of all things. That is true, but it is the kind of thing that we don't necessarily experience all the time. Nevertheless, if I were to say to you, "The spiritual path is about seeing God everywhere," I would mean that not symbolically or metaphorically, but to say we should actually in fact see God everywhere. Now, that is not the everyday experience of most of us, unfortunately. And why is that? It's because we're seeing something different. There's something in the way that hides us or veils us from that. Those things tend to be our own beliefs and conclusions as presuppositions about what the world is and what God is and who we are. Nevertheless, we must try to get past those things in order to see and understand God.

In order to do that, we need two things. First of all, we need belief: a belief founded on revelation. And we need to believe. I stress that because it's a component in the path to knowledge: Believe in order that you may know. But belief isn't enough. We also have to have faith. And in this distinction, I would say faith is defined as acting from and living from that which we believe so that it is in fact a seamless part of our existence.

For those of us who are on the path, what does this action or this life mean, or what does it come down to? It comes down to the spiritual path, which is about discernment and concentration. When I say "discernment," I mean submitting every part of experience and knowledge and belief to the question, *Is this real, or is this illusory?* This is what discernment is all about, and it is a relentless effort. And as we question these parts of our world or these parts of ourselves and find them to be illusory, or not real, they will disappear—because their role is no longer necessary. And finally, what we are left with is just the real.

7

Question: *Recently I have been having doubts about religion. How can you be sure of its authenticity? There are so many arguments about religion, and every one has a proof or a refutation. How can we be certain that we can know God through any religion at all?*

Response: My sense of things is that the answer to your questions is closer at hand than you may realize. The very fact that you are asking these questions demonstrates an intuitive understanding that there is more to the world and to life than meets the eye or that you find in the superficialities of everyday experience. What you are now searching for is a context in which to explain and understand the things that you sense are real.

It would be easy to respond to your questions by saying simply, "Have faith," which as the Bible says is, "the substance of things hoped for, the evidence of things not seen." (Hebrews 11:1) But I think you have passed that point. You truly have a deep intuition that there are more dimensions to reality than you can grasp rationally and, for now, experientially. It is also important that you have seen through the various proofs of God which, in the final analysis, can only support what we understand in a much deeper and intuitive way.

The only way you are ever going to answer these questions is by exploring these things for yourself. You have already taken the first big step in that you are asking these questions. Religion and its interior process, religious mysticism, are here to help you. What these things have to offer you is structure and methods and hundreds (or thousands) of years of a refined process that has been developed in order to help people like you answer questions like yours. This, I believe, is the only serious alternative you have for exploring the interior dimensions of yourself and the world.

Question: *I find myself being wrenched back and forth between the realm of "the world" and the realm of the soul, with a feeling of despair. What advice would you give?*

Response: This being wrenched back and forth between the realm of the world and the realm of the soul is surely one of the greatest agonies and also the greatest indicators of spiritual awakening. In this, your pain is a very good sign. And yes, when you see the glimmer of truth right before you and see the blindness of other teachers to it, there is a further combination of despair with yearning that is emotionally draining. This wrestling with how to reconcile God's creation with God puts you in the company of St. Augustine, St. Paul, Moses, and other great spiritual teachers. It is a sign of no little significance.

You speak as if you are in two minds about things. This is not true. Your experience is that of dealing with these conflicting perspectives, which, as far as I can tell, you are doing in considerable depth. Let your frustration drop away. Deal with what must be dealt with. Look through it, not at it. In all of this, the thing that would be most helpful to you is to have a regular spiritual practice and, beyond that, real tools and instruction in interior work—not in the form of focusing on dogma or exoteric ritual (although these things have their place) but focusing on the respite it provides the soul to make the veil more transparent. This is what religion and the path is all about.

Chapter 2

On Existence and Its Meaning

The Purpose of Creation

WHY DID GOD CREATE THE WORLD? WHAT IS the point for Him, after all? The deep things of God are inaccessible, but some understanding of the meaning of the world and our place in it is necessary. God is infinite subjectivity. How is it that the Divinity could be known? How can infinite subjectivity experience itself objectively?

Let me draw an analogy. Let us say that you are All and Everything. And you wish to be known. How do you draw objective knowledge out of pure subjectivity? Because of your infinite possibility, we can speak of modes, phases, parts, qualities—language fails. But all of these things are you, and are in you. Consider a part of yourself—say, your red blood cells. These are the part of you that's going to get to know you. How can you accomplish such a thing?

Two things have to happen. First, you have to give the blood cells some of your intelligence. That part is easy, because they are all the same substance, all part of you. But then you have to create for each blood cell the illusion that it's separate. And then you have to produce in that illusion an experience that is analogous in some direct sense to the whole rest of you, so that the blood cell, by proceeding and experiencing the illusion that it had before, can understand the correspondences to what is beyond illusion. And then, in this analogy, the blood cell will be able to see and experience, and then through those experiences assimilate those experiences into the knowledge of the whole.

God is all possibility. The human soul exists as a possibility within God. Taking the word "possibility" literally, this means that each possibility of a soul is unique. And as such (but it is also a mere possibility) it cannot know itself as separate from God. In fact, it cannot know itself at all. It simply *is*. It is part of God. It has no awareness of itself as distinct. When that possibility is manifested into the classroom of the corporeal world, this classroom must be structured in such a way that the possibility can know itself. And if it can know itself in a complete manner, it will know God. God Himself wants to be known. You must not think of this as mere information, as merely a fact to be grasped and then filed away with other facts. It is a reality that you must learn by presence.

Corporeality

The soul needs a mirror so that it can actually see and know itself. And so there must, by definition, be a condition created in which the soul can contemplate itself. And corporeality *is* that condition. Only under the conditions of duality and polarity can a subject contemplate itself as object. All of creation, all of manifestation, all of life, and all of our experience—all these things—exist solely for the reason and purpose of allowing *you* to know yourself and to know God. That's why everything exists. Creation exists so that you can experience the world, and through that experience see the resonances of the inside of yourself, and recognize the Self[5], or God. That's why we're here. That's why all experience is for us. And that is what we should be doing with each experience.

The Knower

One of the great Names of God is The Knower: He who knows, He who knows everything. What is it that God knows? We know from the sacred writings that in the beginning was God

5. Self is the one universal infinite subjectivity that defines the basis and essence of all that is.

and there was nothing with Him. He had no partners. And later we are told that God is as He was, again without partners.

So what is this knowing that God knows? Clearly, the answer is that God knows Himself. But what is this knowledge, and what does it mean to know something? This is important, particularly for those of us who are on a path of knowledge, where the notion of knowing becomes central. What is it we really know? Clearly, we have a lot of information about things, but that's to know *about* things. And we have to distinguish between things we know about and things we really know— because to really know something means that we know it existentially. We know it in our hearts. We really know it, not merely about it.

Let's take one of the fundamentals. What does it mean to be conscious? God is conscious and knows, with consciousness, Himself. What does that mean to us? Ask the question: *Are you conscious?* The answer is immediate and clear: *Yes, you are conscious.* You're here listening to me speak. You know that you are, and you know that immediately and directly and without references to higher authorities or to consulting books or foot-notes; it's something that you know immediately. It's that kind of immediate clear knowledge with which we must examine every part of our lives and everything in our thoughts and beliefs. Otherwise we will only have ideas and beliefs instead of knowledge, instead of knowing that which is.

Clearly, one of the problems we have in our particular exis-tential state is that we're surrounded by things, and we know things and objects, and we know about them. What we don't see is the Divine Presence, the Divine Consciousness, within which all of these things live. But if you look around, you will see that what you notice are objects—not the space in which those objects exist. It's very easy to see things, but it's much, much more difficult to see the space in which they exist.

For example, here's a glass. In this glass there is space. But we don't see the space. We know it's there, but we don't see it. How can we see and know this space? This is how: by filling the space. When we do that, the space becomes clear to us, and we can now see that which we didn't see before. This is not simply a clever demonstration. This is how it works. And if you would know the Divine Presence and the Divine Consciousness, you must fill your life and your consciousness and your space and your thoughts with the Divine Name, with the one, true, real presence. And it must be everywhere, and you must fill everything you are and everything you know with that one true, clear presence.

Question: *Why do we exist at all?*

Response: Within the context of most formal wisdom traditions, I believe the question is, generally, answered in approximately this way: By Its nature, the articulation of the potentiality of Divine Infinitude, there is a hierarchy of Being that necessarily emerges—crowned with the Absolute, Godhead or Essence, which is simplex, a unity, thence descending to the domain of Divine Ideas, which form a one-many, neither absolutely unified nor separable, and thence to becoming and manifestation, the domain of multiplicity.

Yet, running through and under all of this is the Divine, which grounds everything, contains everything, animates everything. The multiplicity is both real from one perspective and completely unreal from a higher one; both perspectives must be kept in mind. This is very clearly described in Mahayana Buddhism, in its doctrine of Two Truths: The lower understanding is that there are people, they are in ignorance and bondage, and they must strive to attain enlightenment; the higher understanding is that there are no people, no ignorance, and no enlightenment— there is only Emptiness, or as a Vedantin would express it, the nondual Reality.

The question is: *Why should this be so at all? Why the articulation into manifestation, the creation of human beings, the necessity of revelations and prophets and sages and teachers? Why doesn't the Divine have the good sense to stay put and not stir up a bunch of trouble by creating—well... us?* To this question, the answer I can offer is that we appear to be a modality of the Divine Self-knowledge. After all, you might ask, when a sage comes to knowledge of God, gnosis or unveiling, isn't this just God knowing God? Yes, exactly so, but in a different modality than that of the Divine Self-knowledge at the level of the Absolute Itself. These ideas can be expressed in religious language: In Islam, God says: "I was a hidden treasure and loved to be known."[6] The same idea can be expressed in almost mechanical language, as in Plato's statement that it is in the very nature of the Good that the Good expresses or communicates Itself; that is Its nature.

Question: *What is the contrast between what we sense is true and what we usually experience?*

Response: It is the difference between the reach and the grasp. It is the longing to be home. It is the reason Odysseus returned to Penelope. It is who we are. If an institution exists, and if it is part of your experience, you have to deal with that as you do with all experience: You have to see it for what it is, and you have to decide what to do. If you seek to change an institution, you must do so with all the effort and skills you can bring to the task. You must do so with a determination to the excellent completion of your objective. The task must be done with all the intelligence, integrity, honesty, and selflessness you can bring to the task, because, ultimately, the thing that gets changed is you.

How you go about what you do is how you open the door to intellection. This is the actual arena in which the path is

---

6. Arabic: (كنزأ مخفيأ) is a Hadith Qudsi that has a very prominent role in Islamic mysticism and Islamic philosophy.

conducted. You see, you act, you observe; and if you pay attention to what happens inside you, and search your soul for the things you find, you can come to know yourself. You may have a desire to reject things or to render them meaningless. This is an error. No-thing is meaningless. Things actually *are* the meaning. God has placed us in a world of things and actions. Everything has a purpose. All of existence, all of phenomena—and all of manifestation itself—exists *only* so that you *personally* can see and do, so that, *ultimately*, you can know yourself. There are no accidents. Everything that is has meaning. There is nothing to escape from.

Chapter 3

On God as Our Guide

GOD IS OUR GUIDE, AND WE CAN REPOSE IN THIS knowledge. This is the ground of faith. But you can no more abandon your will than you can abandon breathing. You have to take every step you can, on your own, and use the best judgment you have. You always have the obligation to do that which is best, but there are no guarantees about the outcome, except that it will provide you with experience. It is for that experience that you exist; and it is through that experience that you can come to know yourself and, through that, you come to know God.

You have to stay awake and pay attention and do that which is best at every step. So long as you do, God will not abandon you. This is all we are allotted, but it is sufficient in order for us to find peace and, God willing, some intimations of what lies ahead. But you cannot ask to be certain that you are doing God's will. You will never know. You can never know. The question is meaningless. Do what you can, do it for the best reasons, and do it now. The rest is in God's Hands. You have done your part. Be at peace. Rejoice.

Knowledge as a Veil

The intellectual sets out on the path to God armed with much information, seeing that what we know is not merely a collection of useful facts, but real metaphysical understanding about reality, religion, tradition, good and evil, and God Himself. This person is a scholar, and has been brought to religion through spiritual literature. This intellectual approach to religion is not a false starting point. It is, however, only a starting point and nothing more. Philosophical and metaphysical

16

understanding are invaluable, especially for those whose entry point is intellectual or scholarly.

Yet even doctrine offers its own trap and can become a hindrance, a distraction, or worse yet, a corrosive element that is antithetical to the work of the spiritual path. At worst, the spiritual quest is degraded into a philosophical exercise, and the intellectual, who should know better, ceases even to actually think, falling instead into the practice of quoting other people's thoughts, which bounce around like so many pebbles as they are catalogued as interesting tidbits of rhetoric. This sort of activity can be carried out endlessly, but it never leads to the slightest amount of knowledge of the deep meanings behind every lived moment.

The world is a classroom, not a debating society. Our job is to learn to see and hear the significance of every unique lived experience and let that meaning progressively remove the blinders surrounding our souls and raise us to a level of knowing that makes all things translucent. The knowing that we seek is a knowing of ourselves. Self-knowledge does not come from books. Even the dazzling explication of spiritual literature carried to the highest level is worthless for our spiritual development. On the Day of Judgment, God will not ask us what we know about Plato, Meister Eckhart, or various philosophers; He will ask us *who we are*. We will not be able to answer in terms of comparative metaphysics or give the answers we have memorized from the sages. We will have to give our own answers.

Therefore, one of the most difficult parts of the path is that of learning what we know for ourselves as opposed to what we think we know just because we can answer questions. Only the answers from ourselves and our own experience are worth anything. Nothing we have learned from books can come with us to Paradise, for our answers cannot be stated in terms of another's understanding or experience. We have to know for ourselves, and we have to be that which we know.

No one gets to real knowledge by mastering the thoughts of the sages. You can steep yourself in the most interesting, thrilling, incisive literature our species has produced. But it is all beside the point. No amount of studying Plato can be guaranteed to provide any real insight; it may, but so might gardening; so might caring for the sick. These are all activities that, given the contours of the individual soul, may prompt real insight. It is our job to take in hand what we have and to poke, prod, and push it in ways that it needs so that it may break free from its dream. This requires great courage and ruthless objectivity.

The alternative is hypocrisy. To attain insight requires stepping beyond the library and into the heart. It requires a transformation of the self. It requires taking more risk than most are prepared to take, more self-scrutiny than they are prepared to tolerate, and more openness than they can stand. Yet, this is the very stuff of the path to God. The reason people fail on this path is not that they lack the brains, but that they lack the courage.

Hope and Resignation

Nevertheless, we live in the world, and it is here that we must see and understand and plan and act. We have no other choice. Action is everything, for only in our actions do we have a chance to make the symbols real by working with ourselves. So we think and plan and try to do good and try to live a virtuous life with a view to a higher truth and harmony.

But in all this we must recognize that there is a constant intertwining between our planning and God's planning and that ultimately God disposes. We try to plan for our future, and that is our duty. We try our best, but at the same time we should combine our intention to plan with an attitude of surrender to God. In not knowing the future and in doing what is right and doing our best, we can know peace—as peace reconciles hope and resignation, best efforts and trust in God. It is in this light that we work in the world: We do our duty, we do what we can, and we do our best.

The spiritual life is not to refrain from doing those things at all, but it is to remember that in the trajectory of our life, which means the past, the present, and the future, the only point of action that we have is the present. We must do what we can, and in our doing try to discern the mysterious interplay between our actions on the horizontal plane and the Divine Action, which is a vertical causality (an effect in this world whose cause is transcendent to this world); and we must try to discern how the two enmesh together to weave our life.

In this warp and weft of existence, the critical point, the only point where we have free will, is in the present moment, in the now. We cannot act in the future. The past has already gone. The past and the future are in God's Hands, and He has given us one choice among the past, present, and future to act, and that is the now. Further, in a miraculous and mysterious way, our attitude determines the future, both ours and the world's.

Question: *Why doesn't God give us what we want?*

Response: We pray for many things, both material and spiritual. And sometimes it seems that God doesn't answer our prayers. Sometimes we are sure that we are asking for something He wants us to have, like the grace to resist a temptation or the ability to forgive a wrong. So we wonder: *Why doesn't God give us what we want?*

Let us look at that question carefully: *Why doesn't God give us what we want?* I am going to set aside the "why doesn't God give us" part and focus on "what we want" and ask: *Do we really want what we are asking God for?* How can we tell? What we desire is what we put our hearts and souls into. If we are asking God to give us something good, but we don't care enough about

19

that thing to do what we can to get it ourselves, then how can we say we really want it?

It is true that everything comes from God and not our own efforts. We know that, and we must not forget it. The point is not that God needs our help to do anything—and it is not that we can do anything without Him. The point is that without the desire, we are not asking at all. Asking without desire is like standing at the door and forgetting to knock and wondering why you're not being invited in.

Asking means wanting, and wanting means trying to attain. God doesn't need our effort, but our struggle joins our desire to His action. This is true of anything we ask God for, but most especially when we ask Him for spiritual knowledge. How can we claim that we sincerely want knowledge of God if we are not willing to pay? What is it worth to us? How can we expect God to give us enlightenment if we are demonstrating all the while, by our lack of attention to it, how little we really want it?

So, it's clear that in order to truly ask God for spiritual knowledge, we must first want it. The question now becomes: *What is it that stops us from truly wanting the spiritual knowledge that we ask God for? What prevents us from truly searching for God?* The answer I propose to you is that you cannot search for something you think you already have. The biggest block to gaining spiritual knowledge is believing that you already possess it.

Question: *I have been told that everything around me is there for my own personal experience. How so? How is the physical world both real and unreal? How does one wake up every morning knowing there is a "huge movie set" out there but still pretend it's real? Sometimes I see through the "movie set" and also through people's intentions, and when I do, I feel detached. Sometimes I am carried away as if it were all real.*

I was told that I should not get carried away because it is as if

I was not happy with the current state of things and want to change the world. Astaghfiru-llāh ,[7] *my intent is not to be ungrateful. Sometimes there are situations that call for some reaction or else one is taken for granted. Isn't that what free will also means?*

Response: Your description of the world as a "movie" is really quite accurate. As the Sufis say, "The world is an illusion, but the truth is always being shown there." So, you see things pretty clearly. The world is real, and it is unreal, much as it is both One and Many. The real question you are asking here is: *Why did God create the world the way He did?*

We can only have partial answers to that question. But from our point of view, it has to do with our agency in allowing God to know Himself. We are here to know God, and the process by which we achieve this is through knowing ourselves. Knowing ourselves can only occur through experience, which requires the creation of a world in which to have experience. That is our job here.

As you continue to mature in your practice, you will be able to find more peace in this knowledge. But as you are relatively new to the path, some of these contrasts can present themselves as quite jarring. Never mind. The world is the world, and your task is to see it for what it is. This is a journey that is going to last the rest of your life. You are off to an excellent start. Yes, of course, some situations require action. That is part of our responsibility, too; this is also part of knowing ourselves from our experiences. In all cases you must do and say that which you determine to be good and right and true. You must act in accordance with your understanding.

But what you must *not* do is assume that you know the final end or outcome of an action. We have all seen examples where

---

7. *Istighfar* (Arabic: اِسْتِغْفَار) is the act of seeking forgiveness from Allah, usually by saying *Astaghfiru-llāh* (Arabic: أَسْتَغْفِرُ اللَّهَ), which means "I seek forgiveness from God."

an action made with the best of intentions turns out badly. Similarly, we have all seen seemingly impossible problems resolved in a way that is a blessing for all. These things are in God's Hands, and we do not know the final purpose of anything, so we end even our most fervent prayers with "May *Thy* will be done."

So do your best, speak up, do that which your conscience directs you to do. Then leave it in God's Hands. But above all, and in all things, be true to the path and the invocation[8] of God's Holy Name. That is your greatest help and refuge in this complicated, fragmentary, and problematic world. This will help you stand apart from the flux of the world and the cyclone of events around you. Continue to try to see things objectively and from the "outside."

Any effort to say prayers ritually, in any form, will be a blessing to you. In this connection, I would like to stress that it is important to keep up the regularity of your practice; this is much more important than any particular technical aspects of practice. So, say your prayers on time as best as you can. Continue to say the invocation. Try to make the rhythm of all the rites part of the fabric of your life. In time this will become one of your greatest strengths and the bedrock that underlies the flux of daily life in the world.

Try to lean up to the great objectivity that includes all. Only God's Awareness is able to absorb all the things that the world can heap on us.

---

8. In this book the term "invocation" means repeatedly calling upon the Name of God ("Allah") while being fully present.

Chapter 4
On the Spiritual Path

The Path, Discernment, and Humility

What is it that brings us here? What is it that brings us to the path? For most of us, it's really the sense that we are somehow incomplete. Sometimes this is described as a nostalgia for Paradise. But at root, it's the sense of incompleteness that is really the part seeking the whole: the whole, of course, being the One God. We sense that deeply, and we also sense that it is possible to know the whole. And we accept what is sometimes called "the mystical proposition," namely that the Divine can be known personally, or directly; that the part can know the whole. I hasten to add that the word "holy" means at root "whole." So, how is it we do this? We do this by taking up a path. And a path, by definition, involves traveling. If it didn't involve traveling, it would be called something else: a system, or a school, or a teaching.

We must constantly and relentlessly interrogate our experience and our ideas and our world outside ourselves and within ourselves, so that we can find what is true, so that we can examine our beliefs, and so that we can proceed from illusion to reality. In doing that, we abandon all of the things that can't come along, because falsehood can't be part of unity. We learn about ourselves and about the world. Some things that we think are prerequisites for the path turn out to be things we learn on the path or gifts from the path. Take, for example, virtues: A virtue is not something that can be learned in principle or that can be understood theoretically; a virtue must be learned existentially, and it must be practiced.

Perhaps the best example, and perhaps the key virtue, is humility, because it is with the God-given grace of humiliation that we learn what is true and what is false. And when we in ourselves examine the features of existence, or our ideas, or the things around us, and subject those to the lens of discernment and objectivity and concentration, we learn what is false, and that is a humiliating experience. This reminds me of the famous anonymous prayer, "Oh Lord, more of Thee, less of me."[9] We know it's often said that the saint is someone who is empty of all but God. This emptiness occurs from our discernment and abandonment of the things that are false, and the things that we have taken as true that aren't, or the things that we have accepted but have not demonstrated in ourselves.

In this process, however, it is possible to mistake the process for the real work, because the real work is the discernment and concentration, and the constant effort to understand and to apply that discernment and concentration and objectivity to everything in our existence and everything in our lives. Otherwise it just becomes a process.

Discernment and Concentration

"Discernment" is a word that has wide-ranging meaning for all of us in the spiritual life. Often the path may be reduced to the formula of discernment and concentration: discernment between the real and the unreal and concentration on the real.

Now, one of the reasons discernment is so important is that we're generally so bad at it. For example, if our discernment were perfect, we would see at every moment the Divine realities. We would understand immediately that we are part of the Divine Unity. But we don't see that, because our discernment is faulty. So how did it get that way? Well, partly it's a matter of paying attention, but more often it's a matter of actually believing things that aren't true. And if we examine our beliefs and interrogate what it is we think we know, we will find our

9. Quoted in the hymn by Theodore Monod (1875).

way to things that are in fact truer. The most basic example is the assumption we all make that we are somehow separate from everything else—this separate identity is something that we seem to take for granted, that is given to us and handed to us, but of course it is false, because we're all part of the Divine Unity.

Practicing Discernment

So how is it that we can perfect and practice our discernment? Well, one of the things we can do is to use our minds and our brains to help us. The mind is on one hand the greatest barrier and your greatest enemy, but on the other hand it is your greatest ally. And not only that, the mind is the place where we all have to start, because that's really where we are when we think about ourselves and the spiritual life and what we would do to make this transition. So, it's good to include the mind and not oppose ourselves to it.

The problem with opposing ourselves or opposing our mind is really twofold: The first problem is that it focuses on and acknowledges that which is bad or untrue or is an adversary; and the second is that it strengthens that adversary with every effort of opposition. So, it is better to work with the mind than it is to oppose it.

Now, one of the things that's true about the mind is that it has characteristics of a sponge, and it absorbs all of the objects and experiences and activities that it comes into contact with. And just as if you squeeze the water out of a sponge, it automatically refills itself with air, so the mind wants to be full. It wants to be active. And so often it makes much more practical sense to use this natural tendency and to go with it rather than to oppose it.

So the thing to do is to present the brain and the mind with things that are higher. This is what sacred rites and meditation and invocation really do. They present the mind and the brain with something better with which to occupy itself, and something that leads to a higher place and opens out onto a much great spiritual reality. And in the process, a kind of inversion takes place, as it usually does between ontological levels. In this case, in the world, all of the objects of experience distract us and take us away from our center. All of the items of intentional practice pull us together and lead us to unity and to God. We want to fill our brains and our minds with these true sacred activities, the primary of which is of course the invocation, so that they will help us in this process.

Now, we don't all have the time to start our day with a long period of invocation. I would suggest to you that one of the things you can do to imprint your day is to make sure that you have brought yourself together and you know who you are and what you're doing and affirm the practice for yourself—just so that you can make that affirmation to yourself. And then let that carry you through the day.

To speak of discernment is to raise the questions, *What is there to discern?* and *Where does this discernment take place?* We can look around and see that the world is full of objects and people, and for that matter interactions. And we respond to these with our own understanding of them or our own assimilation of them. And this is very subjective. This is from the nature of who we are as individuals. And the union of the objective and the subjective occurs in what we call experience, which is really one of the great miracles of existence. Why should there be experience? What does it mean? Clearly, there's much to be discovered there on the spiritual path.

Now, often we are told that we should not seek experiences, particularly spiritual experiences. And that's for several reasons, not the least of which is that we don't want our spiritual lives to be governed by our imagination, and we don't want our imagination to present goals for the spiritual life.

Also, experiences can be difficult to understand, and they can sometimes be misleading. But what we're really focusing on is not *an* experience, but experience as such: We are changing the focus of our awareness from the object to our experience *of* the object, which is necessarily internal.

Now, this is a very important point in the spiritual life, as we begin to fathom and explore our own interiors. The interior life is something that draws us in, and if we allow it, it continues to build and continues to draw us in further. And one of the ways we allow this is by examining this very question. And as in all things, there is the invocation to help us and be with us in this process.

There are two occasions that I'd like to focus on. One is that if sometimes you are invoking and this idea occurs to you about examining the quality of your experience, it's good to take a moment and do that. Another occasion—and this happens to all of us every day—is that suddenly at some moment we realize that we're not invoking, that the invocation which in principle is perpetual has left us and we've forgotten it. Now at that moment, you should thank God, because you've seen it. You've seen this occur. And then return to the invocation and put your attention on this very process. You will find, that in those moments when you have suddenly remembered, when something has called you back to the invocation, that you are more present at that moment, that you're more awake at that moment, and that's just the kind of moment that you want to take to ask this question where you explore your own experience.

Asking Spiritual Questions

When a question arises, one of the things that we might do is run to the library and look at all of the research about that particular question or topic. This is particularly true for those of us who like books and like to do research. However, there's a trap here in that the soul is much more comfortable finding out what a scholar's opinion is on a topic rather than facing its own self and what may or may not need to be changed in its own substance. Asking other people questions is important, and those other people can give you answers. There are two parts of this process that are important. One is formal and the other is informal. The formal process is that by asking a question, no matter who you ask, you at least get to formulate the question and objectify it so that you can see it more clearly. That's a very useful step.

Then subjectively, you ask a question to a spiritual authority. By "authority" here I mean simply someone who knows more than you do about the topic you're asking, not necessarily someone who has a formal title or position in the hierarchy, but anyone to whom you would go to ask a particular question. Asking that question is in many ways like a prayer, because you're really asking for God to fill in a particular uncertainty with a particular certitude. And in simply asking the question, you put yourself in the position of both humility and faith, given that you're open to whatever that answer may be.

Now, when you get that answer, there are a couple of things that may happen, and I'd like to say here that in many ways, getting an answer to a spiritual question is probably the worst thing that can happen—because that tends to close the door on that question, and we tend to look at that answer and polish it and put in on the shelf right with its kin, and be done with it.

Instead, when you receive an answer to a question, the thing you must ask is: *Am I changed?* Does this answer transform you? Or does it ask you to do something differently or in some way change? That's generally the measure of a question being answered. Consistent with that is the notion that a question that is answered will certainly lead to other questions, and this process continues to unfold as long as you ask the questions and your soul continues to benefit from the process. In that process, you have to always use discernment and try to interrogate all of the things that you hear and all of the things that you think about yourself, constantly questioning and testing what you think you know, what you think you believe, why it is you believe that, and so forth. All of this is an important and integral part of the path and of growing in the spiritual process.

From the point of view of the spiritual path, the answers you seek will not be found in other texts or in the works of the saints and sages of history. These are the answers we must find in ourselves. In the spiritual life, and particularly upon an esoteric path, it is terribly inviting to think that a question can be answered, and what's more, that there is a right answer, and that we can find it in books. This is the kind of easy deception the lower soul seeks. It wants to resolve the pain of the question by applying an answer rather than confronting itself. Perhaps the answer is in Meister Eckhart, perhaps it is in Shankara, perhaps Rumi. The ego would much rather spend its time finding out what others think instead of weighing and meditating and invoking with the question.

At this point, you have pursued answers to the questions you have asked, and you have found some answers. Perhaps you are satisfied and think you have come to terms with these things, to some degree, at least. But, let me ask you a question: *Now that you have some answers to these questions, have these answers transformed you in any way? If so, how?* Again—and I see this kind of thing a lot—it is all too easy to settle for answers instead of understanding. It is tempting to seek an answer in order to satisfy some part of the soul that feels insufficient without the answer. But the answer to a spiritual question must not simply be a new acquisition of information for the lower self. Real understanding will not feed the part of the soul that has the question, but will cause it to die a peaceful death. There should be less of us rather than more of us after the answer. But this new understanding must be revealed in your soul by God, not from the philosophers.

This is how it works: When we confront a question, we must examine the question in as much breadth and depth as possible. Then we must look inside ourselves for the keys and resonances that can provide insight. Our work in doing this is not to find an answer that will satisfy the question, but to find a key that will reveal the answer by restating it or by seeing it from a higher level. Spiritual questions are never answered at their own level. Nor are they satisfied with information. The process is to explore the question, not to search for an answer. Spiritual questions are not mere problem-solving. A spiritual question is a prayer that God may reveal truth within us, transforming us in the process. God's response is not to the question, but to our spiritual need. This is why so often the answers we need are not ones to the specific questions we ask, but they are revealed in the process of our asking. God always gives us more than we seek.

When we find a real answer, it will not simply "seem right"; it will reveal the question in a new dimension that will be clear to our soul. That will allow us to answer the question with certitude, if only to ourselves. If we can't speak from our own soul, and if we can't speak with certainty, why speak at all? That is why I gave you the answer that I did.

Now, in terms of answering the question you actually asked: A phenomenon may appear at a particular time with some aspect of its nature predominant, at a particular level (on a particular plane), in relationship to other phenomena. The "sense" of this is a matter of being sensitive to these various qualifiers and contexts. It is also a kind of sense we gain from experience in navigating such things, like a sense of direction. An often-overlooked aspect of this is that the soul, the subject, engaging with these (objective) phenomena, is doing so from some corresponding part of itself. That part also exists with a nature, on a level or plane, in relationship with and in proportion to other parts of the soul.

A true "sense of natures and planes," requires a sensitivity and familiarity gained from navigating the interior experiences and states corresponding to the objective phenomena being considered. This requires that we learn to observe our interior states objectively, including their changes, since they too are phenomena and not our true selves. In short, the sense requires self-knowledge at least as much as metaphysical knowledge. The subject and the object do not arise independently.

Spiritual Travel

The notion of traveling is kind of a strange concept, because it involves traveling some sort of distance. But really, what kind of distance is there? We want to go somewhere perfect, and we want to be somewhere eternal. Perfect and eternal: The Divine Name is perfect; the current moment is eternal. We already have what it is we would be traveling to. So the question is not really, *what is our goal for the future?* but, *What is our goal for the present, and how can we bring it as much as possible into the present to make it available to God so that the Name can be present to us?* Because regardless of what has happened in the past, regardless of the trials, the errors, the baggage that we have in the past, every moment is new and perfect, and every invocation is a new beginning. And we should see it as such. It is perfect and it is eternal, and it is here, now, one.

As travelers on the spiritual path, we often encounter the question: *Are we actually traveling?* It's an important question. Often people come to the path with the idea that the path is like a train that goes to Paradise, and entering the path is like buying a ticket on that train. There's a certain truth to that, but it's not a very practical and helpful way to understand the actual working of the path. Similarly, there are many who see the Divine Name as a kind of charm or talisman that has a power of its own, which of course it does have; but that concept doesn't really require anything of the seeker.

In fact, there's a reciprocity here. The Divine Name is the way God makes His presence known to us. Our invocation is how we become present to God. As we do this, we also work the path. As we use discernment in our everyday lives, it becomes clear that there is a stumbling-block, a significant obstacle, in terms of treading the path and assimilating knowledge. It is ourselves who are that stumbling-block, that obstacle. We somehow need to get ourselves out of the way of our own progress.

Let me illustrate this with a traditional story. Let us say that you grew up in a country which had overcast skies one hundred percent of the time. There were clouds everywhere all the time. All you could see is clouds. Then one day as you're walking along, for some reason there's a wrinkle in the atmosphere of some kind, and there's this patch of blue. And you see it. And what you say to yourself and what you say to all of your friends is: "I saw it! I saw a blue cloud!" That's what you would think it was. And then later, if you tried to pay attention and tried to perceive the world around you and ask the questions that we are all enjoined to ask as travelers, you might find another opportunity to see another blue cloud. And yet, you might also travel to some other part of the country or part of the world where the sky is not so overcast, and you would see that it isn't a blue cloud at all; it's the sky. It's the one solid, blue, ever-present, empyrean reality that exists beyond the world of the clouds that we usually see.

In making that observation, you have a kind of realization—and realizations on the path don't generally come as lightning; they come more like the dawn. A realization is more like a successive discernment in the process of learning about the world and the path. That's why we have to struggle every day at every moment at every point with our own selves to ask the questions: *Is this true or is this false? What is real and what is unreal?* Because if you think about the cloud example, there was nothing wrong with your perception. You saw it just as it was. The problem was with your belief.

So as we tread the path, we have to question what it is we see, every day at every moment—what it is we think, what it is we feel, what it is we believe—so that we will finally come to know that which is true. So, that's the question: *How do you know that you're traveling on the path?* One question you might ask is: *Are you regularly, constantly, continually, or occasionally confronted with new knowledge about yourself or your world or your environment or your senses, for you to apply your discernment, and exercise that discernment?* Because discernment is not a tool of the path; discernment *is* the path.

Let Knowledge Become Experience

I would like you to think about the questions: *What was it that brought you to seek answers to spiritual questions? What have you found during your travels?* and lastly: *What is it that you're seeking now?* Various paths have different styles and flavors, including the paths of knowledge, devotion, and works. But let's think about that knowledge for a minute. What does that actually mean? What's involved in that term "knowledge"? Some would say there's knowledge in books. There's knowledge in texts. There's knowledge in spiritual talks.

I submit to you that all of that's false, and there is no knowledge in books, and there is no knowledge in texts, and there is no knowledge in spiritual talks. What you find there is information. But in order for that information to be knowledge, it has to encounter a subject. When the subject encounters the knowledge, then it becomes real, and it can live. But without that subject, it remains sterile and abstract. There is a magic in the fusion of subject and object. But that's what experience is.

33

Every experience has that magic to it.

And as we approach the path, we try to make the potential knowledge real and living knowledge through our own experience. That's why the rites are so important, the practice of the invocation is so important, the virtues are so important: It's because by those actions, this potential knowledge gets to live and be real within us. Try to be as aware as you can, to pay as much attention as you can to your own experience as you encounter these things in your life and in the path. Try to be as aware as possible, as present as possible, so that you can give to God all that you have.

Inner Authority

One way to conceive of the spiritual path is to say that it has three parts, or maybe three pillars: doctrine, tradition, and method or practice. Doctrine is important because it conveys the truth. And it's also beautiful and encourages us onward and encourages us in our practice. But more than that, doctrine also has very practical value in that it allows us to validate and sometimes gauge or even calibrate our own personal lives as we move forward on the path.

Tradition is important, certainly, because it preserves our contact with the Divine, and it gives us a space and a civilization in which to live and practice that will return us to the Divine. And it also provides the keys to a practice and a method. And that's the third pillar: the method. Now, these things are different in that the first two, doctrine and tradition, come to us from the outside. And practice, or method, is connected with our own personal experience and our own efforts to live in, submit to, and be participants in the Divine process.

The first two have the danger of the possibility that we can only know these things theoretically. It's all too easy to accept formulations—in fact, beautiful formulations—for something that we actually know internally. I think we've all had the experience of saying to ourselves: "Well, do I really know this, or do I just have a lot of words about it, and other people's explanations?" Certainly, those explanations are helpful and beautiful and provide guidance, but unless we know things personally, unless we have them in our own experience, they remain theoretical.

And so, the practice is the process of making that which is theoretical real in our own hearts and in our own lives. And I think it's fair enough to say, although it may sound excessive, that doctrine and tradition aren't sufficient. Because they are insufficient, there is what we call esotericism; there is a mystical path. Mysticism is the proposition that we can know the Divine directly. This is part of this triad of doctrine, tradition, and practice. This process is the process of the remembrance of God[10], because the remembrance of God has all of the elements. It has the Name, which is the truth, and it has the invocation, which is practice and participation in these things, because without that practice, and without making these things internal, they remain theoretical.

These things are all important and need to be brought together in our lives: the doctrine, the tradition, *and* experience. When they are together, then we have wisdom. Then we have presence and the possibility of knowing the Divine directly. And in that process, we all come to recognize that we have a kind of internal spiritual authority, which will grow over time and which cannot be ignored, under pain of falsifying ourselves. Yet with that knowledge, we have also to use the wisdom of the doctrine and tradition to bring these together in harmony and in synchronization. When we do that, we have the full path and the wisdom that the path offers. But without that, the doctrine remains just words.

---

10. The remembrance of God is similar to an invocation, an act of calling out God's beautiful names with presence and not mechanically or by rote.

Spiritual Authority

Spiritual authority: Where does it come from, and who has it? Now, it's easy to say spiritual authority comes from God, and that's certainly true. But that answer isn't necessarily helpful practically. Let us approach this from the other direction: Who has spiritual authority? Do I have spiritual authority? Does the pope have spiritual authority? There's a preacher near me in the city who's railing every Saturday evening and Sunday morning about sin: Does he have spiritual authority? Some time ago I saw a program on television about a man who I believe is in Guatemala who says that he's the Second Coming of Jesus, and he has quite a following there. Does he have spiritual authority? If you pursue this question deeply, you will inevitably discover the truth, that spiritual authority comes from you. It's what you give to someone else. And in turn, you accept their authority over you.

Now, there's a lot of room for question in that process, and since by definition you're looking for something you don't have, or something to make you bigger or better or more complete—how do you find that? In many ways it's like the old joke that anybody who would go to a psychiatrist needs to have their head examined. There's a real truth to that. Similarly, anybody who would go to a guru must be lost.

So how do we find and determine where this authority can be, so that one can benefit from it? When you find a teacher, there are formal criteria. As travelers on the path, we love formal criteria. We want to make sure that our teachers are part of a tradition, that they have a chain of transmission and their practices are orthodox. Those are the formal criteria. But there are informal criteria as well. We also need to make sure that our teachers really understand our soul and our problems, and not only that, that they themselves are honest and that they're not self-interested or careless. When you satisfy both the formal and the informal criteria, then you can give yourself over to a particular teacher and be obedient to the things that teacher offers.

You still have the responsibility, and forever will, of knowing what's in your own soul and heart so that you can benefit from whatever exposure to guidance you have. In medicine, it's a matter of saying to yourself: *Am I getting better?* And if you're not getting better, you need to go back to the doctor and get a different pill. And if that doesn't work, maybe you need to find another doctor.

Similarly, in the spiritual life, you say to yourself: *Am I more centered? Am I more at peace? Do I feel closer to God? Do I feel more in harmony with the path and the practice?* And if not, you need to go back to your guide and say: "Something needs to change," and maybe be given a different exercise or a different practice, or some other discipline that will help you. And if that doesn't work, then maybe you need to find another guide. Spirituality is often the practice of finding other guides. There's no one-size-fits-all solution.

So there is this absolutely imperative process, this interplay between authority and responsibility, where we always have to examine our soul and say: *Am I receiving the nourishment I need, and what can I do with the help of my teacher, or teachers, to get that nourishment?* That's a difficult question and process sometimes. Once upon a time, I was able to ask that question of a great spiritual master. And his answer was this: "Paradise is on an island. To get to that island, you need to take a car to the train, and take the train to the city, to get the plane to take you to the port, to get the boat that takes you to the island." And so it is.

Question: *How is our spirituality affected—or how should it be affected—by society and the political and economic systems we live in? Are some times more conducive to real spirituality than others? If so, should we try to bring them back?*

Response: The issue of spirituality is not one of restoring a former state of humanity. Humanity's state is a constant one. Spirituality is about the individual—you. The human soul manifests all possibilities. Some will never rise above their mistaken devotion to the material. In other words, they will never realize truth. But the world is perfect for its intended purpose. It is theophany.[11] It is a classroom for the individual soul, which may seek and find God even on the factory floor, in the nursery or the office, for God is ever-present.

It is true that "good," in these times, is nearly synonymous with "getting," not "being," and with "appearance," not "embodying"; but it is a mistake to blame capitalism and, more important, it is irrelevant to do so. We might equally blame atheistic communism, or dictatorship, or any other social construct. There are many people who are "good"—whose actions are informed by moral values and virtues, and who surmount the onslaught of the temptation to settle for situational ethics or self-glorifying greed.

In the end, what the world or what society does is immaterial. All that matters is the state of your own soul. No esoteric tradition, not Kabbalah, the esoteric tradition of Judaism, or Christian mysticism, or any other can be fully effective without its exoteric context, for the inner meanings of the outer word of God are equally present in that outer world. The sacred scriptures speak to the soul that is open to its message, and do not speak to the heart that is hardened, and many highly intelligent seekers mistakenly assume that God's literal words conveyed through the prophets have no relevance to their quest for intellectual insight, because they assume it is not a book for the highly intelligent, but for the common man. This could not be further from the truth.

11. Theophany is the manifestation of a deity in an observable way. In this context, theophany refers to God made manifest and recognised (known) by itself.

Changes need to be made at the individual level, and so education, the fostering of a culture based on higher principles, and, ultimately, a relearning and dedication to the sacred, to Scripture, to the saints and sages, and to doctrine and metaphysics is necessary. The world of metaphysics and esoteric doctrine is not open to all; it is hermetically sealed and only open to those who have a sense of the sacred and the personal affinities and capabilities to understand these complex and subtle principles.

There is a world of wonderful esoteric doctrine from great religions. In this connection I would like to recommend the classics of this world: Meister Eckhart, Sri Shankaracharya, Honen, Black Elk. There are many others. How clever of God to have hidden the truth in religion—who would think to look for it there!

Question: *Why is it so important to follow one spiritual tradition?*

Response: So far as I know, all authentic esoteric paths are not concerned with research on exploring new ideas on the nature of reality. These paths are exclusively concerned with using the revealed doctrines of religion in concert with methodologies both revealed and refined over time to bring our entire being into harmony with reality. All of these require that we belong to a revealed religion with an authentic spiritual tradition.

If a flying saucer were to land on my front lawn, and beings were to step out and offer the knowledge of an advanced civilization, it would be necessary to say: "No thank you; I have to get back to my prayers." This is because there is nothing of any ultimate significance they could offer. The ultimate questions about existence and meaning have already been answered by the Buddha, by Jesus, by Lao Tzu, and by many others. Our task is to pursue that teaching back to the source.

Perspectives and relationships between different ontological levels are a means for gaining (on the intellectual level) a more complete conception of the Whole. Keep in mind that each conception within a particular defined religion is integral to itself, and in that sense, comparative religion is of no real utility in gaining spiritual awareness. Comparing is a reductive, dialectical process, whereas seeing, hearing, and knowing are non-linear processes. You can incorporate neither Hinduism into Taoism nor Taoism into Hinduism. They are similar only in terms of the fact that they are both attempting to describe the indescribable. When we pursue a path within any form, we must accept the method of description as it is, knowing that it will be, by definition, incomplete and imperfect because human beings cannot explain God. If they are fortunate, they may, however, experience the revelation of truth, and this is the purpose for every single one of the forms.

Question: *You say that there are aspirants who are not candidates for the path because they are not courageous, that they are not willing to take risks. Take risks of what? Of subjecting themselves to discomfort or pain?*

Response: We cannot decide to subject ourselves to a risk of pain. The effort to do our best to raise our soul must be approached not according to whether it will be painful or not, but regardless of the very idea of pain. There is no way to avoid either God's grace or God's trial, and we experience both every day.

Question: *Where does one look for an authentic spiritual path?*

Response: There continue to be a few possibilities still extant in the modern world. In terms of Christianity, I do not know if it is still possible to find qualified interior instruction in the Catholic Church; however, because of its vast size, I imagine that direct interior instruction from a master of gnosis may be available somewhere, if we can find it. In terms of the Christian

Orthodox church, I have reason to believe there are still a few gnostic masters available; most would be in residence on Mount Athos. A full monastic life would require a vow of celibacy, but it may be possible to take instruction from a qualified guide without having to live in a monastic setting. In terms of Buddhism, I am sure there are authentic masters available in Zen and other forms of Japanese Buddhism as well as in Tibetan Buddhism, although authentic Buddhist masters of gnosis may be equally difficult to find among the clutter of modern Buddhism. There may also be other qualified teachers elsewhere.

Question: *How can one find a teacher who has reached enlightenment? And how do teachers determine whether a seeker is suited to their particular path?*

Response: You will find in your search for the truth someone like Bob Smith. Bob had a very powerful experience, changed his name to Swami Bogusananda, and now says he can teach you to transcend your own blindness and limitations so that you, too, can experience Reality/Illumination/Enlightenment/ the Beatific Vision/etc.

Now, there are several possibilities here. One possibility is that Bob is a fully enlightened being, because "the spirit blows where it will." Another possibility is that Bob is a complete fraud and charlatan, in which case he will waste your time and money. The third possibility, and far more likely, is that Bob, for unknown reasons, has had an experience of genuine Awareness. History seems to be full of such events (for instance, Blaise Pascal). There are many examples of this phenomenon, too.

The problem is that, even though Bob's experience is genuine, he cannot understand it in a way that is helpful. He cannot situate it in terms of a doctrine that expresses who he is and what the world is. Consequently, he may have had a very individualized and fragmentary experience that he has taken for full enlightenment. But what is more troubling is that he may not have access to the doctrinal or methodological resources that can facilitate his teaching to others.

Buddhists say about themselves that they have had 2,500 years to work out the process and, through that process, people have transcended themselves and have come to know. This is a powerful argument, particularly when compared to Bob's case. Such things are occasions for trust or prompts for faith. It's like hiring a carpenter to build a house. We have two candidates: One of them has a certificate from the guild, and the other has no such background or certification. Yet this doesn't tell us which one can actually build a better house. I always tell newcomers to the path to stick with an orthodoxy: not because it guarantees anything—it doesn't—but because it is a hedge against wasting their time and lives.

Anyone who is attracted to a path, its master, or its method and understands its perspective is, in general, a candidate for that path. Beyond this minimum threshold, everyone deserves the benefit of the doubt. What I am describing here is not the entrance criteria, nor the particular set of gifts and experiences that are required of the fully realized spiritual wayfarer, but what it actually a means to engage the path and work the process. Accordingly, when evaluating a potential candidate for a path, we must attempt to discern characteristics of the individual that have the potential to allow efficacy of that path for that individual.

Certain paths will not be efficacious for everyone who wishes to be a candidate; there must be a nature that is, at minimum, not locked into exoteric type dogma, a constitution that is in a state of inquiry rather than deception or desperation, and a reasonably well-balanced mind with some inward orientation. These are not easy things to determine from written material, which is why we prefer to sense the soul in person, preferably face to face. Some should be directed to stricter exoteric paths, not to a path that requires inner fearlessness and willingness.

Question: *What should my attitude be toward all my failures on the path?*

Response: Don't be too hard on yourself. Looking back at your errors is a tricky business; did you expect to find none? You have always known you have made mistakes of various kinds. But it is also important to remember that this leaves out the other side of the story: that you have done good and noble things and many deeds that are virtuous, all in the very same life.

Furthermore, it is not productive to focus only on errors of the past. (It is worse to focus on errors of the future, but we can deal with that later.) The straight path is marked by intention, gratitude, repentance, and humility. By repentance I do not mean hyperbolic vows such as: *I will never ever do such-and-such again;* and there is no small amount of egoism in saying: *I am the worst of sinners.*

Have confidence in yourself. Have trust in yourself that you can come to a better place. You can do this!

All you have to do is to drop away the veils on that knowledge and it will come pouring up. You already have an intimation of that; you're just afraid you might fail.

Also, be careful about assessing the impact of your own work. That kind of assessment is a tricky issue as it involves one of the deepest questions in philosophy: the polarity between good and evil.

Question: *What is involved in following the spiritual path is more like weeding out the weeds in our soul and opening up the garden of our self to the light of the sun. The image of a patient gardener, pre-paring his soil, carefully selecting what he will plant and what he will take out of his garden is much more realistic for most of us than the warrior storming the gates and exposing himself to annihilation* *in a superhuman quest. Is this a correct understanding?*

Response: The soil of our self cannot be prepared; it is what it is. We doe not pluck the weeds and plant the flowers. It is more that we recognize a weed and refuse to give it water.

Question: *It seems to me that there is one central principle that makes the spiritual journey arduous: The closer one gets to truth, the less company one has. Like any natural hierarchy, the hierarchy of wisdom is a pyramid. Therefore, it has a broad base that narrows as it gets to the top. In this sense, God is not the slightest bit democratic.*

This principle creates all kinds of personal difficulties. Primarily, it means that the more you learn about the way things are, in an ultimate sense, the harder it will be to deal with the world around you, in a practical sense. It may even be dangerous to your health, for if you let on too much of what you know, people may try to stone you, in one way or another. It is also painful in other ways. If the main joy in life is loving relationships with others, then, paradoxically, the closer one gets to truth, the more difficult it will be to maintain loving relationships. After all, it is difficult to love those who are trying to stone you, particularly when they are trying to stone you for telling them the truth. This raises a key question: What do we owe those who would stone us?

Another problem is that, as you ascend, you can only look back down at where you have come from. So at any one time you are more or less blind to what is coming. This means that you will be blind to what those ahead of you know. Likewise, all those below you will be blind to what you know. Consequently, the higher you go, the more you will be living in the land of the blind. It will further become more difficult to get others to see what you know, particularly as you can never admit to the existence of the pyramid itself, or your own place in it. The result, once again, is increasing separation from others. The closer you look into a person's interior, the less chance you will have of finding common ground, placing your relationship, past or present, at risk. This leads to another key question: Should we cast our pearls anyway? *We are counseled not to, but as the binding force, truth is love, and thus, in this sense, withholding truth is withholding love, which is purely counter-productive.*

So, you speak, and others stone you; you don't speak, and you stone yourself. The spiritual journey is rife with paradox.

Response: There is a pyramid whose point is balanced on the point of another pyramid. The base of the lower pyramid rests on the earth; the inverted pyramid opens up and out. As you ascend the first pyramid, yes, it narrows as you go higher. Yes, it distances you in a certain sense. But at its apex, this reverses because at its apex is where the transformation of the soul enables you to know what theophany is, what Love is, and that it saturates—absolutely saturates—the entire pyramid you have climbed. It is the point at which you see God in everything. It is the point at which you are compassionate toward everything because you share in the indescribable totality and passion that God has toward everything, even those who stone you; and you also have transcendence of knowing that it does not matter if they do; this is the point at which you will do God's will because you have no other will. And if His will is that you tell what you know and be stoned for doing so, it will have no effect of any kind on your embodiment of truth. The base of that inverted pyramid is measureless and boundless and never ceases opening up. But it is not foreign territory; it is your veritable self.

As you rise you will feel this opening up. In Sufism this is called "intellection". Elsewhere it is known as awakening, enlightenment, and gnosis.

Chapter 5

On Prayer

On the Primacy of the Invocation

ALL OF US ARE HERE BECAUSE OF A KIND OF spiritual longing, because we understand in some deep and principled way that we are incomplete, and much of our lives is driven by this longing to be complete. Finally, the notion of longing is false, because it requires an object; and we all know that there are no objects. But between here and that kind of realization, longing serves a very important purpose. Longing is an encouragement and a reminder to refocus, to always return to the one thing needful. And for us, the one thing needful is the *remembrance of God*.

The remembrance of God is our practice and our life and is more important than any of the other activities that we might engage in, regardless of how spiritual they may seem. There's a place for all those things. There's a place for doctrine, which is true and which is beautiful. There's a place for art. There's a place for virtue. But none of these things really have the place in our lives that the primacy of the invocation of the Divine Name has.

God gives us His Name and is in His Name, and it is our role in creation to remember His Name and to pronounce His Name, and to do that in the forefront of our conscious awareness every chance we get. And if we can't do it in the forefront of our conscious attention, it must be in the background.

Now, we all live in the world. And God knows that He has placed us in a world that is difficult and complicated, particularly at this moment in time and history. But that's irrelevant. Our job is to remember Him and to pronounce His Name. And we need to do that at every moment, using the tool of discernment to always be asking the question: *Is what I'm doing more important than the invocation of the Divine Name?* Because even though there are many things that are important to us, and that we must do because we are in the world with our lives and our families and our studies and our children, the question must always be asked because the lower soul has such a tendency to run away with us. It has such a tendency to be distracted by the world, by things that are frivolous and even by things that are sometimes honorable and noble.

But throughout all of these things, our obligation is to use the tool of discernment to ask at every moment between this activity and that activity, between this word and the next word, between this thought and the next thought: *Is this the invocation of the Divine Name? Is this worthy of taking my attention? Or should it be back on the remembrance of God?* It has been said that the remembrance of God, the Divine Name, the invocation, is a kind of boat that carries us from here to Paradise. That's a good analogy. But it's a boat that has to be rowed. And we have to be asking ourselves the question: *Am I rowing?*

Remembrance of God: Not Vain Repetition

The remembrance of God is at the very heart of our spiritual practice. But what does it mean to invoke, really? Is it a matter of keeping the Divine Name in your head and on your tongue? Yes, it is. But it means ever so much more than that.

A couple of years ago I attended an art exhibition of classical calligraphy. In the collection was a group of calligraphic forms that were done in the form of birds. And I thought; *Well, that makes perfect sense: Birds are certainly a symbol of freedom, and they fly in the air, and they're beautiful, and we've all heard about how they symbolize angels or higher states.* So that made perfect sense to me. But a little further on there were a couple of what seemed to be fairly humorous designs, calligraphic Divine Names and sacred formulae that were done in the form of parrots. I couldn't quite understand that. I thought about it, and finally it occurred to me that this was humor, and that what was going on was an attempt to poke fun at those who invoked like parrots, in shallow form, without any real understanding, without having the Name really in their interior and their hearts.

In the Bible, Jesus speaks of "vain repetition," (Matthew 6:7) which is clearly a possibility. The perfection of remembrance requires the totality of the one who remembers. There is much to be understood here, and much depth to be plumbed and to be experienced. And it is helpful to approach that with as much understanding as you can so that the practice opens up in its depth. There are many ways to do that. For the moment, let's just look at the language. The term "remember." Remembering God. Remembrance of God. What does the term "remember" mean? What is the opposite of "remember"?

The opposite of "remember" is "dismember," which is what God does. Unity dismembers Himself in order to create you and me and our experience and the world and all of creation. And our task, the work we have taken up, is to re-member God, to refer everything in our hearts and our lives and our experience back to Him from Whom it comes. That is our role in this process. And it is in some measure the most important work there is and, in many ways, the only work there is.

Being Present in the Invocation

The Name of God of course is perfect, and our response to it should also be perfect. Our task, therefore, is to be as present as possible, to bring as much of ourselves as possible to this act of remembering God and pronouncing His Name. In order to do that, we need to be as present as we can, because our awareness of the presence of the Divine is often the presence of our awareness of the Divine. We need to be as present as possible.

Now, how do we do that, and how do we know that? One way is to ask yourself: *Am I fully present?* and if the answer to that question is anything other than certitude, then you're probably not fully present. How do we become present? And very often the answer is that we bring ourselves to things by removing the obstacles that stand in our way; that we bring to the invocation more of ourselves and less of the things that tend to distract us. When we invoke, we need to be as present as possible, and not bring all the kinds of baggage that we usually carry with us in this journey.

Let me give you an example. Let's say you're walking through a forest. One of the ways you can walk through a forest is by noticing everything, by saying: *Ah, that's a pine tree. That's a squirrel. That's a chipmunk. That's a flower I don't recognize—it's beautiful.* And so forth and so on. And in the process, you can make your way all through the forest and never really have the experience of being in the forest, because it's so easy to let ourselves be carried away with this horizontal string of associations and facts and inputs and sensations and thoughts and memories.

Instead, we could take a fixed stand and simply be open to the Divine Presence, which we know is present there all the time, as it is here and now. We know that the Divine is present; the problem is that we're not. So, in this example, how do we make this transition? How do we become more present? The answer is, with the path. The first element of the path is discernment: discernment between the real and the illusory. And on this journey, if we pay attention and we interrogate our experience and the things that come to our minds and ask the question: *Is this real, or is this illusory?* we will come to some understanding of what the difference is. When that takes place, we can concentrate on the Real.

But it starts with discernment, and discernment needs to be practiced everywhere. When we practice this discernment everywhere, we can slowly begin to dissolve this veil of illusion that surrounds us. Often we hear about "piercing the veil" as if it were an act done with a sword, and suddenly the veil is rent, and reality stands before us; but that doesn't happen very often. What usually happens is that, as we make this journey, if we try as hard as we can, if we exercise our discernment and be as present as possible, slowly we can begin to unravel the veil, one thread at a time. And every opportunity we have to exercise our discernment on our experience, we can dissolve one more tangle. And then suddenly—or slowly—the veil disappears. Because it wasn't really there: It was a mistake. That's an overwhelmingly powerful and in many ways difficult thing to imagine, but it is the very essence of the process that we have taken up. In this process discernment is everything.

Integrating the Body and the Mind

Seekers' tendency to separate themselves from the world can often be seen even in the temptation to distance ourselves from the body, especially when it comes to prayer. To do so is a spiritual mistake. The bodily element cannot and must not be separated from the mind. You should not think of them as separate, but as parts of the integral whole. Because of the union of body and soul, every religion requires practice. It would be a grave error to confuse practice with meaningless rote ritual, because the very purpose of practice is to discipline and integrate the mind and the body, and the efficacy of practice depends upon the mind's focus on that integration. It is to our entire being, not just our minds, that religion is addressed. Consequently, it provides physical rituals for our body and objects of devotion for our feelings, as well as doctrine for our minds.

All of life is practice, or can be, if you pay attention. The problem is in remembering to do the work, both interior and exterior. There are things that can help. God has provided them for this purpose. It is important to recognize that the opening of the Eye of the Heart[12] can be experienced as an emotional or even bodily reaction. It is the mind's recognition, expressed through the body, of your longing for God. It is something you want with your entire self, not just one part of it. This is the point of action and ritual. In prayer, the pronouncing of the words themselves carefully, knowingly, and intentionally has a power that you must allow yourself to recognize.

It is typical for seekers to reject this emotional and bodily element of prayer. They have reservations about allowing such experiences free rein. They often hold back because of fugitive thoughts that they might look silly or be embarrassed by such a naked act as praying sincerely. This degree of intellectualism is perfectly illogical. The physical accompaniments to prayer are not an emotional or psychological accident.

Say a prayer. Say it silently or aloud, it doesn't matter. Pick a prayer you know. Say each and every word slowly, consciously, and knowingly—even a small word like "the"—and know, as you say it, that this word's meaning is deliberate. Try to understand that every word has meaning and that none of the words are accidental. Do not allow your mind to chatter in the background with multitasking or a running commentary on a lot of personal issues. Clear it. Act as if you are addressing Something that is beyond your ability to comprehend. Something that does not even think like you do, does not exist like you do, does not hear with ears or see with eyes, is not human at all. Something that owes you nothing; Something you have the temerity to address and acknowledge—respectfully, because you are beneath notice in terms of that Something with respect to its powers.

Don't apply any of your anthropomorphic ideas: Just say

12. In this context, the Eye of the Heart means direct and unmediated experience of reality

the words of an existing prayer. Don't make up a prayer of your own. Don't beg. Don't ask for world peace. Don't complain about the state of the neighborhood or demand that your sore toe get better. Just say the words, without brain-chatter, without motive, without wondering if you're silly or undignified or a hypocrite. Just do it and be sincere in acting as if the Something is real and has all those characteristics.

When you're finished, don't think at all. You will find this hard to do. Try hard to remain unthinking for at least a full minute or two. Now think and think with precision and care. Don't make up "correct" thought or literary thoughts or explanations or self-analysis charts. Just re-experience what the qualities and nature of the experience actually were, second by second.

Such a prayer must become a daily practice. Make a distinct break with your daily routine. This daily practice must be precisely the slow, intentional, knowing offer of a prayer to God. A prayer should never be rote in any way, because you must always be aware that your words and your desire for the peace are true and honest and that you are addressing the Something that is so powerful that people go down on their knees to do it. *Every* part of practice is meaningful. A person who goes to his or her knees or prostrates should be in a state of recognition of the One whose reach and grasp so vastly exceed the human realm, such that we are humbled before It. You need to pray: You should not put this aside for any intellectual reason whatsoever. There is no one stopping you from this practice: not the world, nor modernity, nor social convention.

I would like to bring your attention to one of the greatest spiritual classics, *The Way of the Pilgrim*.[13] It's the story of a nineteenth-century Russian pilgrim who discovers in the New Testament, in 1 Thessalonians, the phrase that we must "pray without ceasing." And he sets out on a journey to find the

---

13. *The Way of the Pilgrim* is widely available to purchase and can be downloaded without cost from a few websites.

various spiritual authorities in Russia at the time and ask them what that means.

One of the masters discusses the issue of distraction, and he makes the point that there are distractions from the left, and there are distractions from the right. Distractions from the left are the usual kinds of things we think of as distraction: I'm preoccupied with the notion of what I am going to be doing tomorrow afternoon, or what kind of agenda I should have for the meeting I'm going to, and so forth and so on. The usual kinds of things.

But he also notes that there are distractions, as he calls it, from the right. And those are things like: *Am I saying this prayer correctly enough? Am I standing in the right place? Am I using the right tone of voice?* The point is that those things can distract us from the purpose of our activity just as much as trivial things can. There's an analogy to be made directly in terms of the spiritual path, which is to say that it can be all too easy to let the mechanical process substitute for the real substance of the rite, or to stop simply at the symbol.

Look around you. Look at the people we see here. And you will say to yourself: *I see a person.* What you don't say to yourself is: *I see this person's face.* Because you know there's more than what is simply being represented by their face, and you understand that. Similarly, if you think about who you are and what this process of knowing yourself is, it doesn't really do much for you to be able to look in a mirror. It can be all too easy to substitute the symbol for the reality, or to stop at the symbol, or to let the mechanical process of conducting a rite—even a rite like the invocation—keep you from plumbing the depths that are available. Because a rite like the remembrance of God really requires all that we are. It requires that we bring to it all of our substance, all of our attention, all of our intention, in order to do this properly. And so it is with the invocation, and it is possible to let remembering to say the Name act as a substitute for actually participating as fully as possible in the remembrance of God.

Question: *I had an interesting experience while praying. It was extremely emotional, and I felt like welling up. I felt like I was pushing through something; like something was cracking. I felt a release of pressure that brought tears to my eyes. I ended up feeling a strange peace. My rational mind is trying to find the reason behind this experience.*

Response: You have had an important experience: the phenomenon that took place when you prayed to the Father. The body's reaction, which you call "emotional" as though emotions are a bodily element, was in truth the mind's reaction, and you describe it as a "welling up." This is the recognition, by your mind, expressed through your body, of the longing you have for God.

Further, you say: *I felt like I was pushing through something; like something was cracking.* This very strong response is precisely the beginning of the opening of the Eye of the Heart. Now this is something you want with your entire self, not just one part of it. This is the point of action and ritual. The pronouncing of the words themselves carefully, knowingly, and intentionally has a power that you yourself recognize and that has clearly been missing from your life. This is the opening of a door.

It is not considered "fashionable" by intellectual minds to pray, and therefore someone who is instructed as to how to properly do so often holds back because of fugitive thoughts, of looking silly or being embarrassed by such a naked act as praying sincerely. This degree of intellectualism is perfectly illogical. You felt, "a release of pressure that brought tears to [your] eyes", and you say, "I ended up feeling a strange peace." These, too, are the signs of your entire self and your entry into the indescribable power of opening yourself to God. It is real. It is not an emotional or psychological accident. It carries with it, both for the initiate and for the beginner, a certain uneasiness because it is so powerful.

You do not need a community of the wise in order to seek God. This is always an individual path. You instinctively know what you really experienced. This is what I want you to do: Learn a sacred prayer and say this prayer three times each day. Make this a distinct break with your daily routine. Find a quiet place, clear your mind, and pray. When you say the prayer, concentrate on the meaning of every line and of the relationship between the nothingness that is you and the Totality that is God. As you recite this prayer carefully, knowingly, and intentionally, try to reach up to the high state you found before. Don't force this; just relax and focus your attention and try to lean up toward that high state. Don't expect anything from God, but expect yourself to deliver the prayer to Him with concentration, sincerity, and humility. That is all you can do, and it is what you must do. Anything more is up to Him.

You should say the words and concentrate on their meaning. Do this prayer and do it regularly. There is much more to come, but I think you are ready to start. This is the place to start. There is nothing stopping you from making this a daily practice. What I mean by this is, precisely, the slow, intentional, knowing offer of a prayer to God. You do not need a community or to travel to find like-minded travelers. Many around the world live in isolated places and situations. You do not need to go anywhere to find anyone. You are where you are. And you have Him. The name makes little difference. Buddhism may focus on His being beyond comprehension, no-thing or void. But this is not His only aspect. There is also similarity. And He is not indifferent nor lacking in sentience. You will learn the meanings of these inadequate words in time and will leave behind the anthropomorphic conceptions you have learned.

Question: *I prayed a perfect prayer yesterday morning. I was just in a state of calm serenity. And it dawned upon me that my prayer had been perfect. Does every prayer partake of perfection, no matter how distracted or distraught one might be in the course of it, if it is performed intentionally, and not in one's sleep?*

Response: You have taken an important step. What's more, you received a sign from God about this: the fact that you gave no thought to its perfection until it dawned on you that your prayer had been perfect. This dawning is a little hint that you're on the right track. Further, you say: *In some ways it was simple and unremarkable and I realize that I have prayed perfect prayers, or prayed perfectly on other occasions, but without reflecting on its quality.* This is an extremely significant statement. It reveals, in you, a beginning awareness that you didn't have previously; it is the awareness of the meaning and importance of small things, of what you have called "the ordinary." This awareness is very significant.

Now, we need to talk about some other elements of "perfect"—elements that I want you to think about and incorporate into your assignment of praying a perfect prayer. And for this, you will continue to hold on to the qualities of your experience and continue to include all of the elements that were part of it: the intention, the care and attention to the rituals, and the clearing of your mind.

In your description of your perfect prayer, you describe a number of external conditions: the sun, the flickering light. Does the perfect prayer have anything to do with the corporeal conditions in which it occurs? Let's say the house is quiet and peaceful. You don't have sore feet, and you are located in the calm serenity of your own house or, perhaps, a sacred space. Are pleasant conditions necessary for you to say a perfect prayer? If so, why? In other words, could you pray a perfect prayer where the conditions have no relevance whatsoever?

To answer this during your effort to pray a perfect prayer, you will have to go deeper into who you are. If I tell you to go to the verge of the nearest highway or the median of a busy intersection and pray a perfect prayer, what does your lower self say? Does it say: *I can't?* Is perfection so contingent upon the conditions under which you are praying? I want you to pay even more attention to the conditions and to why those are seemingly important.

The second element of "perfect" I want you to consider is intent. Intention is not and cannot be a factor. If intent were a factor, its opposite would exist, and that would be an unintentional prayer. Can someone unintentionally perform a prayer? No. You *decide* to pray or not to pray. And when you pray, the key requirements for partaking of perfection are sincerity and humility. You don't partake of perfection by intent. Intent is not a word of prayer. Sincerity and humility are words of prayer.

Sincerity and humility are cheap words, though. They are so cheap that people use them all the time to mean "manners" or "politeness" as in writing "yours truly" at the end of a not very important letter. People may declare that they are humble and yet display the signs of self-ignorance, secret self-satisfaction, and hypocrisy in their souls in all the small moments of their lives. The truly humble and the truly sincere do not make such declarations. They *are* such declarations. They *live* such declarations because they know themselves. This does not in any way prevent them from achieving excellence or attaining their goals. It simply places them in the right relationship to God—the relationship that allows their souls to open and to rise.

A prayer is an offering by the nothing to the Something. To offer such an acknowledgment to God is to offer all of our imperfect self in humility and awareness without any idea other than the offering. There must be no element of expectation or reward. To think thus is to think with the ego. A perfect prayer—or any prayer—only partakes of perfection when it is offered unconditionally. Now expand your definition of "perfect" and work on saying a perfect prayer that incorporates these two levels of awareness: awareness of conditions and their irrelevance, and awareness of the inner state, not the intent with which you approach your prayer.

Chapter 6

On Sacred Texts

How to Read a Holy Text

WHEN YOU READ A HOLY TEXT, IT IS CRUCIAL to approach it properly. If you do not, it will be of no use to you. What you need to learn is particularly difficult for anyone who has scholarly training. The problem is that we tend to approach a sacred text with all the critical skills we have learned in school. That will never work. It is like trying to understand love by examining its physiology. That will lead to a mountain of interesting facts and information, but it tells us nothing of the experience. It is like looking at pictures of a dance instead of dancing.

We must approach a sacred text on its terms, not on ours. We have to get ourselves out of its way. Further, we must forget, or at least suspend, all that we have heard about the text from previous commentators, including the saints and sages of the tradition that offers us the text. Those things are interesting and sometimes helpful—but not here. Reading a spiritual text is about your experience with the text, not that of someone else. As in all things, attitude is essential. There are other things that can help:

How to Read - Truly Read - A Sacred Text

This experience is for you alone.
 It is between you and the author of the text
 It is not a literary creation
 It has powers beyond your everyday comprehension
 Your task is to open yourself up to what it has to say to you.
 It will speak to you, to your soul, directly and individually
 This will only happen if you approach it on its terms ...

How to Read - Truly Read - A Sacred Text *(Cont.)*

Stop your mind from talking inside your head as you read
> There must be no words formed in your mind as responses while you read
>
> Do not allow your brain to chatter to you as you read
>
> If you do so, the words will stay dormant on the page as dead ink
>
> Your brain will busily and continuously talk as you read, saying things like:
>> *Oh, that sounds similar to ....*
>>
>> *Oh, I wonder what that means*
>>
>> *Didn't Augustine say something like this?*
>>
>> *I want to ask a question....*

Read with the conviction that you are hearing the voice of God
> It is crucial that you align your entire mentality to this attitude
>
> If you approach the text as "just another book," your mind will give you a running dialog
>
> That will be your ego dissecting the voice of God
>
> It is vital that you cross this mental bridge

Ego versus humility: pitfalls to note and eschew
> If you read as a critic, it will be like thinking you are more knowledgeable than God
>
> You would be expecting God to prove Himself to your ego
>
> Do not even proceed if you cannot adopt a greater level of humility
>
> All you will find is a useless list of things you disagree (or agree) with
>
> All this will be your ego talking

This sacred text exists for your sake
Accept that this book exists for you, to speak to you
It will speak directly, not as literature, philosophy or
history
It will transfer its meaning directly into your being, not
into your brain
It will speak directly if you put your intellect aside and
do not talk back to it

> *Know that you are engaged in hearing*
> *God Himself speak to you*

If a passage says nothing to you
Do not analyze
Pass it by
The text is not of this world
It is directed precisely to each individual and their
condition
It will transmit what you are capable of truly hearing
Accept that you are not yet ready to hear the sections
that seem to say nothing to you
There is no need to seek the opinions of others
It will be of no benefit to parrot the opinions of others
The understanding you need will come to you when you
are ready

When a passage 'speaks' to you
Do not analyze
You will recognize it as true immediately
Mental commentary will be unhelpful
You will recognize a direct statement about yourself
The word "they" always means "you"
It is difficult to read about "their hypocrisy" or 'their
ungratefulness"...

How to Read - Truly Read - A Sacred Text *(Cont.)*

.../ Be absolutely sure that "they" means you
> Your ego will try to say, "It's not about me"
> It is about you
> The word "they" always means you
> When God speaks of "their hypocrisy," "their ungratefulness"
> It is about you
> Your ego will say, "That's not about me"
> It *is* about you
> This is difficult, but essential, to accept

Read aloud and hear the voice of God tell you about yourself
> Recognize the verses that spoke directly to you—mark them if you must
> Stop reading when it is time to stop
> Start reading again when:
>> You have put your mind and its voice aside
>> You are ready to open yourself without barriers to the text
> Do not make notes
> Do not think about interpretations as you read: Be afraid of making such a grave error

Know that you are engaged in hearing
God Himself speak to you

Triads in Sacred Texts

There are many triads that we learn in the spiritual life. Probably the most common is fear, love, and knowledge. These are general descriptions of the spiritual life of the path. There's another triad that Martin Lings explains in *The Book of Certainty*,[14] and he describes these three levels as the lore of certainty, the eye of certainty, and the truth of certainty, in which there is first of all an attraction. We get the sense of the holy. We see a glimmer of the Divine: the lore of certainty. Then we approach what we have seen: the eye of certainty. And then finally, we embrace it or merge with it: the truth of certainty.

His illustration is to look at a moth and a flame. The moth is attracted to the flame: the lore of certainty. It approaches the flame: the eye of certainty. And it merges with the flame, or is extinguished in the flame: the truth of certainty. It's a good description of the spiritual process in general.

One of the things the path offers, as do all religions, is a set of structured rites, and many rites have a formal structure to them. One of the things the structure of a rite offers is a message in and of itself. The structure of a rite, its form, is a message from the Divine in and of itself. A prayer, for example, is not just a collection of random words; it's a part of the revelation. Also, one of the things you can get from structure is a kind of interior freedom, because if you know the rite, if you can do the rite because you have done it many times, then you are free from thinking about the mechanics of what you are doing, and you are free to collect yourself, to be as present as possible, to pay attention and to invoke, and to be completely part of the holy rite.

One of the best examples combining both this triad of lore, eye, and truth, and the notion of the importance of a structured rite, is in a traditional greeting. A traditional greeting has its own form, and we participate in that. After all, it doesn't mean much to conduct a rite and not be present, and it doesn't mean much to greet someone if you're not fully present in greeting them. That's fairly obvious. Now, we greet one another, and the symbol is, we

---

14. Lings, M. *The Book of Certainty*—publisher: Suhale Academy (January 1, 1999).

are one blood. And in doing so, we step beyond duality. We step beyond conflict. We step beyond opposition. And the very definition of a condition where there is no opposition, where there is no resistance, where there is no antagonism—the very definition of that is peace. When you greet each other, think about it as a formal rite. Participate in it as fully as possible. Do the rite as perfectly as you can. Be as present as you can.

The Divine Word in the Revealed Scriptures

There is a clear and beautiful calmness that arises with seeing the world from the center. This is what paying attention and detachment are about. Curiously, this doesn't prevent you from doing anything in the world or in life; in fact, that is the very arena in which this seeing is supposed to operate. You will also find that it is difficult to talk about, except for the quiet and profound joy of seeing things clearly.

But, a word of caution here. You have begun to stick your toe in the ocean of self-awareness. This process continues indefinitely. Further, it is well known that the higher we get, the more interesting the distractions become. History is littered with individuals who have been overwhelmed by a moment of higher awareness and have concluded that they had received a Divine message or achieved total understanding. Undoubtedly, some did. Undoubtedly some didn't. Some of these people have started cults or new religions based on their experience or on the technique that brought them to their insight. This is the reason that I stress orthodoxy and insist that the interior life be situated within the full doctrine and development of a major religion. This is also why individual guidance is essential for the traveler.

You will find that there is tremendous help available in revealed scriptures, the Divine Word. It brings us concrete advice for our lives in the world, it reorganizes our interior, and it provides a view and a method for transcending our worldly selves. But there is more. There is a magic in them, a piece of the celestial harmony from which they came. And so these Divine words are used in prayers. There is also quintessential prayer—that is, the invocation of one of the Divine Names. The Maharishi Mahesh Yogi (whom the Beatles made famous) once said that he could bring the entire world to cosmic consciousness by invoking "Coca-Cola." One wonders about that, but suffice it to say that there are better choices.

Question: *What should I do if I'm reading from scripture, but I'm not finding it inspiring, and instead find reading Ibn Arabi more inspiring than the scripture itself?*

Response: I submit to you that those private intellections and direct glimpses of metaphysical truth are much more important to your spiritual development than your ability to find spiritual nourishment and inspiration from a particular scripture. It makes no practical sense to compare yourself to someone for whom a sacred text opened the door. All that is beside the point. From here on, the objective is to use those very intellectual glimpses to deepen your awareness and your participation in the presence of God. Holy Scripture can facilitate that process (that is what it is for). Yet it is not unreasonable that a particular revelation does not easily turn the wheels of your heart. What is important is that you find the resources and tools that do turn your heart and lead you to the profound insight of seeing the way things are. As I like to quote: *The awareness of the Presence is the presence of Awareness.* A revealed text may not be the most important thing for you to spend time with at this stage in your spiritual development.

Question: *I keep running across the number three in sacred texts. What is its significance?*

Response: The most obvious triad is fear, love, and knowledge. God is One; and the first distinction (well above manifestation) is polarity or duality. Three is often conceived in connection with the Divine uniqueness because it encompasses both original unity (one) and duality or polarity (two). There is thus a new unity that synthesizes original unity and duality. And so, therefore, there is twelve (another unity involving both one and two; and thus we celebrate Christmas for twelve days). We can look to Hinduism and to *Sat-Chit-Ananda*, but that is not strictly analogous to what the Christians mean by the Trinity.

Question: *What are the triads envisaged by Sufism?*

Response: The most obvious Sufi triad is *maḥabbah-makhāfah-ma'rifah* (love, fear, and knowledge), which Burckhardt describes in the book, *Introduction to Sufi Doctrine.*[15] The reason this is not strictly analogous to the Christian Trinity is that the Christian Trinity is a cosmogonic triad. That doesn't happen in Sufism (or, so far as I can tell, anywhere other than Christianity). God is One; and the first distinction (well above manifestation) is polarity or duality.

---

15. See *For Further Reading* section at the end of the book.

Chapter 7
On Practice and Effort

Doing the Right Thing through Discernment

DISCERNMENT IS AT THE TOP OF THE LIST OF requirements for following the path. Discernment is the key to so much of our spiritual lives and so much of the rest of life, too; highest, perhaps, is the spiritual maxim "Know thyself." This is a very important point to make in conjunction with discernment, because that's really the first ground of discernment. Life is full of complicated issues and matters and choices and decisions that we need to use our discernment to evaluate.

Some of the things that we choose to do are very natural. We can talk about natural desires—something as simple as being hungry, which is easily satisfied in a natural way. Then we can also talk about a kind of unnatural or perhaps accessory need that really comes from the lower soul. The lower soul always has as an objective: either its own comfort or asserting its own identity and its own importance. These things can occur in the midst of any consideration and even of the highest spiritual considerations. In following the path, we can't forget the fact that although we've chosen the spiritual path, the lower soul is going to come along for the ride anyway. Even in the midst of spiritual considerations, it will assert itself.

For example, the story is told, and we may know such cases, of someone who is really working very hard to practice all of the virtues, and they're very proud of that fact, that kind of contradiction. Also, the lower soul can appear as a kind of extra player in the scenarios of our life, much as in an organization, and I think all of us who have had any experience in organizations know there is occasionally this person who is really working to assert herself and her own agenda rather than what's in the best interest of the corporation or the body of workers. The lower soul can play that kind of role too.

One of the most difficult realms to evaluate, and consequently one of the richest realms for self-exploration, is in the notion of taking action, particularly when you find yourself in a position where you feel called or compelled to do so. Now, there are many reasons for taking action. We have to evaluate not only the nature of the action, but our motives in taking that action too, because even though the action may be of cosmic importance, if the lower soul is involved, it will try to purloin or co-opt that agenda so that it can assert itself or find comfort in the disequilibrium that's being experienced. The lower soul has really no concern about what is in the cosmic best interest of the world or other people. It is only interested in itself, and it is always only interested in itself. One of the features of this interest in itself is that it's very limited in its imagination. If it feels a particular need, the only thing it will be able to do is to try to satisfy that need rather than replace or balance or minimize the need itself.

Life is full of desires. Some of them are quite healthy and positive. Some of these have to do with the outside world in that we desire to change it or have it be different. It may be that we would like to have a different election result. It may be that we want to change the culture, or we would be happy to change our marriage, or our job—these things are external. Similarly, we have many things that appeal to us personally that we may desire, that we would like to have, and those can be objects such as a new car or an experience or a boyfriend or a baby or recognition or a new job or a raise—all of these things appear in our lives as fairly natural desires. Look at a desire that is satisfied—we all know the feeling of having something that we desire finally be granted, and we feel the ensuing satisfaction. We feel a kind of exhilaration, we feel good, and there's a real joy to having our desire satisfied.

But where does that joy come from? It doesn't come from the object that we've just possessed; it comes from being free of the desire: Because the tension between wanting and not having is finally resolved, and this tension is resolved with this kind of freedom and joy that come from no longer having a desire—or this desire or that desire. That's one of the reasons that poverty is such a key virtue: Poverty is a matter of being empty of desires. We hear that saints are those who are empty of themselves and want nothing.

To want nothing is to be free. It's to be liberated from the notion of wanting or of desiring. That elimination of desire doesn't need to be a kind of ascetic experience or hard-edged resignation to not having; it needs to be a joyous dissolving of the desire itself. When the desire is dissolved, we are liberated from the burden and the energy of having this desire as part of our soul.

The beauty and the peace and all of the goodness and all of the things we seek are available to us right now in this moment and with the Divine Name. That's the context in which we need to use our discernment to evaluate our approach to the things we want, to the actions we would take, to that which we would do or have in the world. Because if this is true, then all of the things are available here and now in this moment. And as spiritual travelers, if we act in harmony together with both the moment and the Name, then the decision will be the correct decision. It may not lead to the kind of overall outcome that we had anticipated, but we have everything we need to have made this decision, and we have been given the moment in which to make it. That's discernment. That's the use of our own discernment in the context of the spiritual life. Acting in harmony with the Name and the moment will give us the right decision.

Tasting the Divine Name

Many times spiritual travelers say that they are not getting enough out of the invocation. They say: "My invocation is dry or mechanical or empty." Now, the orthodox response to that comment is to say, "We are not a path of experiences. And it should be sufficient for you to understand that the invocation in and of itself is the best act possible. This is the act of God, and anything that comes with that in this life or afterwards is a matter of grace. But simply invoking the Divine Name should be sufficient for you." That's true. But there's more to it than that. If you think about it, there isn't anything we have to put into the invocation other than ourselves.

On one level what this comment means is that we all need to be responsible for the quality of our own spiritual lives. It also means that we need to work as hard as we can to be worthy of being the locus of this wonderful act. That's a matter of the practice of religion, and the rites, and the virtues, and everything that goes with the spiritual life.

Now, we could say that the path could be distilled to the phrase "Remember God," and that's true. But there's more to it than that. Because there is a body of knowledge that has to do with the development of doctrines, methods, and teachings that are all aimed at facilitating that very thing: making ourselves worthy and making the Divine present. If you think upon your own experience, you can recall a moment when you really felt gratitude, when you really knew love, when you really understood mercy. If you remember that moment and call forth that moment and steep yourself in that moment and try to remember the flavor of that moment, you can carry that taste into the invocation. It has been said that esotericism is about tasting. There are many things that you can do to bring more of yourself into the practice of invoking the Divine Name. This is one of them.

Self-Witnessing God

To try for perfection in everything you do means to give your best effort. Every soul knows whether or not it is doing so. But to embody that state—the state of bringing the striving for perfection to everything with which you engage—requires *not* that you be aware that "God is watching" but to hold yourself to a permanent standard of striving for perfection *for its own sake.* This is a way to "see" to the heart of Self-Witnessing God.

When I say "for its own sake," what I mean is: If you pay attention to and recognize the quality or feeling that attends giving any act your very best effort, you will find in that moment an expansiveness and a feeling of pleasure that arises from doing your best for its own sake. Conversely, if you pay attention to the sense or feeling that you have when doing a slipshod job, you will find that its content is "gray." You will not have any sense of that which is upward or call it, say, "elevation" at all. "Only you and God know how often you pray and how perfectly." But *you know.* And you already know the sense or feeling that accompanies this. It is a "spiritually downward" feeling, compared to the times when you have given your very best.

These senses or feelings are pointers. The feeling you have when you try your best to do something perfectly for its own sake already evokes a small ray of light. In an esoteric sense, this might be called a "whisper of intellection." Were you to apply the standard of perfection to everything you do, and *not* focus afterward on the imperfections, but only on the experience of having tried your very best, you would have replaced the idea of only doing your best when "someone is watching" with a state of being that would represent embodiment of a virtue of God. And then you would not be asking constantly for a sign of approval from God because it would not matter; you would strive for perfection regardless.

When you interrogate the feelings or state you experience

when you have made the choice to do something sloppily, you will find that it is a not very illuminated state. If you address this rationally, you will always choose to try your best, because the alternative is to experience the knowledge that you have withheld your best; and this feeling is spiritually useless. That which is useful has qualities that raise you up. This does not mean that every act or word or event is done perfectly; it means that you have given it your best, consciously, knowingly, in order to gain the feeling that accompanies doing your best. That feeling is a form of theophany. More importantly, however, it can be spiritually transforming in increments. The downward spiritual negativity that accompanies slovenliness and carelessness can be left behind. Never forget that He is the All-Merciful and the All-Compassionate even though He knows everything about you, because you are His creation. What He wants is for you to raise your own soul so that the veils between you and Him can be dropped.

Question: *How should one invoke the name of God, and what should one expect?*

Response: Simply invoke; never push yourself in this. Also, do not worry about any technical aspects of your breathing; similarly, do not worry about blending one invocation of the Name into the next. Each invocation has a natural end that cannot be avoided. The dividing line between each can be emphasized or not, just as one breath can be held for a moment before it naturally leads into another. Ideally, an invocation should be loud enough for you to hear, but this is not always possible and, in any event, should not deter you from the practice.

But this is all technique; think about the Name and not the technique. In all these things, treat your soul gently and do not be concerned about technical points, nor about your subjective reaction to these things. Relax. Trust God. Trust the path. Trust the method. You have begun a journey that will last forever. Relax and enjoy the journey.

Question: *I seem to think what I am doing in my spiritual practices is not enough. Is there anything more I should do?*

Response: Your problem is one of faith, not practice; this is what could be called "excessive sentimental subjectivism." You should trust in the things God has given you: the path, the Name, the method. You seem to think that these are not sufficient or that they are not providing you with the state or experience you think you should have. This is nonsense. God knows your state very well, and what He asks from you is your best efforts, not a particular result or condition. Further, you are in no position to assess your own spiritual progress. Relax and trust in the things you have. Do everything that is required of you. Try to do a little more. Keep a clean conscience. Relax and trust in the Name, the method, and of course, God. Stop trying to assess your progress.

This, certainly, involves all aspects of your life: home, work, and your spiritual life. None of these things are really separate, and you cannot improve your state by neglecting any of them. That would be to accuse God of not giving you what you think you need. Instead, you must realize that every aspect of your life—every experience you have—is part of the set of things God has willed for you in order that you can learn about yourself and, through that, come to know Him. Simply invoke and trust none but God.

Question: *How do we know when we have done the best that we can versus just shrugging our shoulders and saying, "Well, I've done the best that I can; it's in God's Hands now," when, in fact, we have done something less than the best that we can?*

Response: By your own statement, you already know that you've been a hypocrite when you admit that you haven't, in fact, done your best, and then you make matters worse by saying: "It's in God's Hands", passing the buck back to God, as it were. Every soul knows when it has not done its best. You could not even frame a sentence like the one above if this were not true. I see in your response to this dialog an effort to say: "Yes, I see," and then to put it into a convenient box and tie it up with a pretty ribbon and then go back to the "ordinary life" you have been living.

Question: *I find myself existing in a state of wobble. How does one balance the physical world and the spiritual world?*

Response: You have correctly defined yourself as existing in a state of "wobble." That's exactly right. Now, as to how we go about balancing on this high wire without wobbling, this is almost impossible to describe in words because, in the most ironic and paradoxical sense, words are themselves limited to the expression of polarity and duality. And so, if I say to you that the way to stop wobbling is to jump off the wire whilst still remaining on it, I will sound exactly like a koan giver. That is why koans exist. In their way, the question, "What is the sound of one hand clapping?" is an effort, in words, to crack the mind to a level that is not gained by linear, sequential, rational thought, but is attained by direct intellection, in which we "see" and "hear" without using eyes or ears.

Let me try another way. You must not think of yourself as somehow above interacting with the temporal corporeal world. It is a classroom created for us to learn in and is perfect for its intended purpose. When you read texts, don't read them as literary productions. Eliminate from your mind any trace of "talking back" to the text or engaging in "commentary" as you go. Let the text speak to you of its own volition. Let it describe you to yourself. Let it describe to you the interaction with the world that is both instructive and necessary in order to both engage with it (not merely look at it) and see through it, without making the mistake of thinking that conducting a mental conversation with yourself constitutes an interior understanding or view.

That's the best I can do for you in terms of nudging you forward one tiny, tiny step. Be careful not to confuse your intellectual excitement over intellectual appreciation of cones or pyramids or other symbolic metaphors with the achievement of the priceless gift of actualizing truth within yourself.

Chapter 8
On Living in the World

Using the World as a Mirror

WHEN YOU MANIFEST INTO CORPOREALITY AS a walking, talking, flesh-and-blood creature, corporeality itself presents you with a ceaseless panorama of phenomena. Every single second of your life, you are reacting to phenomena. Every single reaction and interaction is a mirror of you and no other. Your thoughts, your responses, to phenomena are designed by God to tell you about yourself: not to tell you what other people are thinking, doing, or saying—but what is happening with you. That's why it is the small things that bounce you back to yourself.

When we speak of the world as a classroom, created for us as a means of self-knowledge, we are not speaking merely of a good spiritual practice, or a way to make spiritual use of the surroundings in which we happen to find ourselves; we are speaking on a metaphysical level. Corporeality, the world around us in which God has placed us, *is* a mirror for the self. You must understand and see yourself in every encounter you have with corporeality. Every accusation that is made against the other is an accusation that is equally valid for yourself, for the quality of the accused is also an indisputable element of your own soul.

For example, consider the times you think: *I'm better than that*, or *I'm glad it wasn't me*. Every time you react at all, you learn about yourself. Honestly, ruthlessly contemplate whatever is bouncing off corporeality that isn't useful spiritually. When you think, "I'm better," this reaction does nothing for your soul. But, if in the same experience you realize that you have "superiority" embedded particularly in your very substance—*that* is useful.

The object of this game is to recognize and accept what you learn about yourself. The point is not to levy ranks or judgments, but to know, and then to see. And to see is to see the elements in yourself that have no real utility to yourself. When you see how useless this judging of corporeality is, you may come to see that clinging to any sort of superiority is unnecessary. When you see clearly that it is unnecessary, you can drop it from your soul, and light will pour in to replace it. You will no longer need to have it. You will no longer need to pretend you are humble. Humility will be as a state of existence for you, and you will be able to laugh because of all the chains and dross you have been dragging around with you, not even recognizing them in yourself.

You will find you have this power so long as you are not denying truth. Not qualifying it. Not rationalizing it. Not trying to run from yourself. You will know very well indeed that God knew exactly what you were and what you are now. But you will have changed your soul. You will have elevated it. And you will know that was in fact God's objective for you from the very beginning.

If you accuse the world of injustice, you must confront the fact not only that you have practiced injustice, but that both the capacity to do so and the actualizing of that element have occurred many times. And you must know that this is true of yourself. For those who cannot interrogate themselves, the very accusation against the other is nothing other than an ego-claim that you are different from that other. When you say to yourself: *I would love more, or better, if I received more from the other,* you are hiding and failing to recognize yourself as one who rationalizes and constructs conditions that allow you to withdraw love. Under this paradigm, your unhappiness is always the fault of the other. To think that you are an objective, disinterested observer can place you in a position in which you will always and forever consider yourself an exception to whatever you disapprove of. This is not the way.

Seeing Through the World

The world is created as a classroom for us to learn in, and it is perfect for its intended purpose. When you are dragged into daily life in a way that seems to veil the truth, it is helpful to put up no resistance. In fact, that encounter with the realm of the profane should be the very point on which you focus. Don't pull back; go deeper. In other words, if the plumbing is broken, focus every ounce of yourself on fixing the plumbing.

The ability to deal with the world, while remaining at a distance from it, is predicated on the self's viewing the world from a perspective of love. In other words, your "distant" self should view the world as God does: loving it in all of its flaws. Try to see the world as God does. All of the things of the world are ephemeral. All of the things of the world are a classroom. The core of your connection to truth does not go away; nor does it change through interacting with the world. You may think that it rises and falls. That is not true. It is the veil alone that is sometimes dense and sometimes more transparent. Your goal is to have it always be transparent. This is where you will find unchanging Peace.

The goal is to realize that interaction with the world is both instructive and necessary in order to both engage with it (this does not mean merely to "look at it") and see through it. What do I mean by "see through it"? It's an experience that everyone has had in his or her life, often by being overwhelmed with the beauty of nature. It is a moment of unveiling, of seeing what shines through the natural world. Call such a moment to mind and cling to that sense or state you felt when "seeing through" things. Recall it. Savor it. Make it present inside you as a small ember or diamond at all times, and whenever you lose sight of it through engagement with the busyness of living, restore it by restoring the remembrance, until it is pretty much permanently there where you can access it. There is nothing wrong with busyness. It's what we do. The important thing, apart from not beating yourself up yourself, is to tend that little flame of transcendence.

An experience of the grandeur of nature can be like a hammer. But the problem with a hammer lies in thinking that only a hammer can make an impression. To experience transcendence or "seeing through" when you are in the presence of one of God's over-the-top teasers—a soul-stirring sight of the glories of the natural world—can lead to a "thrill me again" mentality. There is a certain spiritual danger in this. As Abraham Maslow said, "I suppose it is tempting, if the only tool you have is a hammer, to treat everything as if it were a nail." The danger is in not recognizing true theophany, which is not limited or episodic, but a step-by-step transformation of your entire perception and awareness.

To attain permanent embodied awareness of theophany is a deeper, progressive journey. It lies not in mountains or rainbows, but right at your feet. But you must learn and practice in order to experience it. I say "experience" it because it is not a matter of seeing it and thinking it is beautiful. Seeing an outer form has a certain judgmental factor to it in which the mind tries to place the object into a hierarchy of being more or less beautiful. But a true awareness of theophany is more profound than that, because it leads to a genuine transformation of the soul, when you realize that you are saturated, drowning, in theophany.

In other words, that memorable experience of the grandeur of nature—the rainbow, the sunset, the mountain—can also be experienced in a dry weed or a maggot on a dead opossum. Pay attention. And what I mean by "pay attention" is this: In those very days and hours and minutes of ordinary living with all its busyness, recognize a moment as it is occurring, when you feel and know a flicker of that very same flame.

If you are paying careful attention, you will find that the

experience of "seeing through" occurs more often than you think. Pay careful attention to exactly what you experience the next time you really laugh. When you learn how (because it is an act of training the mind) you may then begin to see that the experience itself is so filled with "seeing through" that you can begin to recognize more of these occurrences and seek them, because of the quality of elevation they carry.

It is like recognizing a musical tone through the noise and cacophony of everyday life. Once you hear it, you can learn to listen for it. You learn to listen for more of it. Eventually, you can learn how to locate the situation in which it is most likely to be found. And later there may come a time when you learn that you can radiate the quality of that tone from yourself, and not just gather it into yourself, because it has filled a large part of you. At that point you won't be seeing through anything anymore, because everything will be transparent.

In other words, it is a mistake to separate your lived experiences into the two categories of "deeply meaningful" and "banal." Every experience is unique, but that does not mean that experiences are to be categorized as "good" vs. "bad," or "banal" vs. "extraordinary." Such categories are not only purely relative, but completely arbitrary. Once you have applied such labels to your experiences, there is nothing to be learned from any particular experience. It has been frozen and placed in a box along with other experiences that have been given the same label, instead of being drawn closer to be peered into deeply, as though it were a bottomless pool whose surface reflects your self like a mirror. And the label itself carries the hidden assumption that your mental discernment between these opposed categories is superior.

Let us take an ordinary moment. Let us say it's a moment in which your mind says: *She doesn't understand me.* It is a common moment, one that occurs over and over in many people's lives. Typically, this thought is filed as a confirmation that is complimentary to yourself. And it is typically enhanced by a secondary compliment to yourself that generally is framed by the mind as a combination of victimization, heroic suffering, and superiority when the mind says: *I tried*.

Such a convenient and repeated self-justification, of course, makes any possibility of change moot, as well as any recognition of the power to transform yourself one iota. Instead of such characterizations, you must draw the experience closer—much closer. You must interrogate the experience.

Interrogating the Experience:

* What really happened during that moment?
* Did that moment confer a tiny elevation in your heart?
* Did you feel higher? Better?
* Why did your mind cling to this thought, and wrap it around yourself for comfort?
* Does it confer comfort?
* Does it confer peace?
* It this thought useful in any spiritual sense? No? Then why did you think it?
* What does the experience actually produce within yourself? Was it a voice that said you were not "getting" enough from the other?
* Is this state of dissatisfaction where your soul actually resides?
* Why does your soul/mind/ego need that thought of dissatisfaction, when it has no utility?
* Does it produce happiness? If not, then why do you harbor it? Is it because you want to be "right"? Why do you need to be right?

Now take this banal experience to a higher level:

Interrogating the Experience: *the next level*

* Did you once love this other unconditionally?
* Did that experience have different characteristics: qualities of joy, peace, selflessness?
* When did that change?
* How did it change?
* Were the steps from love to toleration just as ordinary?
* Were they also small moments of disappointment that you were not "getting" enough from the other?
* How did those small moments become so powerful they overwhelmed that love?
* How did those small moments become so powerful when each one of them was so small, so lacking in significance?
* Why did you make the decision to record them in your memory?
* What is the utility of the long list of disappointments?
* Disappointments that you carry next to your heart, that weigh it down and harden it?
* Is that logical?
* Were there other choices?
* Are you now a prisoner of this useless baggage you have chosen to carry?

And now take the meaning even higher:

Interrogating the Experience: *the highest level*

* How does this ordinary moment reveal your soul's relationship to God?
* Are you "tolerating" God in a similar fashion?
* Is your mind/ego lying to itself that devotion to God is a different matter?
* Do you think that you offer a special love to Him?
* Is the mind/soul/ego harboring a secret list of disappointments there too?
* What are you offering God?
* What can you offer Him if you cannot learn to embody unconditional love on the corporeal plane?

To love is to give, not to get.

To love is to banish, one small moment at a time, those moments and their content that have no utility to the soul.

To love is to decide that you will neither tolerate nor recognize the thought of being disappointed in the other.

To love is not to allow the moments that take your soul downward.

To do this toward a particular single human being—to become the giving—therein lies peace, joy, serenity, and the sacrifice of the ego that brings freedom. And to do so without thought of reciprocation or reward, but to do so for its own sake—to look into a human other's eyes and see God there—that is to see. To learn to see as a personal state of existence is to transcend the corporeal.

People are used to giving thanks for good things. There is nothing wrong with that, because it is important to recognize and be grateful for good things. But one who has progressed further knows God must be thanked for *everything*, unconditionally and without reservation. Only by accepting everything and seeing the meaning and theophany behind *all* experience on the corporeal plane can you know with total certainty that God is real. Creation is a classroom, and it is perfect for its intended purpose.

Many think that seeing a rainbow is all there is to theophany. Admiring a rainbow is easy. But seeing a rainbow does not produce transformation of the soul, nor knowledge of the self. When you have encountered and plunged into the deep mirror of your ordinary lived experience, nakedly, honestly and without ego—that is when the light begins to glow, the power to transform yourself begins. When you learn how to love, then Love in its true brilliance and power will make Itself known to you.

Ordinary moments of envy, self-pity, hubris, boredom and fear could serve equally as examples of moments that offer knowledge of the self as well as the opportunity to use the rational mind to dissect them, without canned judgment or labels, without thinking you can change yourself completely in an instant, and without applying conventional psychobabble. The point is to discover the depths of their meaning and then begin to make choices and decisions that allow the soul to shed whatever is useless and meaningless from your mind and your life.

But of course, nothing is truly useless or meaningless, for the world is a classroom for the soul. You cannot hope to learn or obtain insight in an instant. Yet you should be confident that you *can* learn, and here, the self must relax a bit in order to let meaning penetrate your mind, without your mind scurrying about in fear that you will be seen as flaky or otherwise weird in the process, or that you have not come up with the right answers.

None of this comes naturally to the person who is accustomed to thinking that the way to reach God is to distance ourselves from the world. This desire to withdraw from the world comes from the ability to see clearly what a mess the world is. And it is a mess. But it is also perfect. Understand—to realize—that the world has only one purpose: All of creation, all manifestation, and all of your experience exist solely for the purpose of your knowing yourself. You cannot escape the classroom by running from it. You can only transcend the classroom by coming to understand why, if you were God, you would have created the world precisely as it is.

A common reason for the desire to escape from the modern world is that it is meaningless. This is an error. No thing, no experience, is meaningless. Things *are* the meaning. God has placed us in a world of things and actions. Everything has a purpose. All of existence, all phenomena—all of manifestation itself—exists *only* so that you *personally* can see and do; so that ultimately, you can know yourself. There are no accidents. Everything that is has meaning. There is nothing to escape from.

Harmonizing the Interior and the Exterior

We all know that God is One. On the other hand, we live in a world. And when God creates this world, He does so in sets of polar opposites, and we all know them as good and bad, black and white, up and down, male and female, day and night, and so forth. As it says in the second poem of the *Tao Te Ching*,[16] we know that beauty exists only because we know that ugliness exists. Similarly, sound and harmony accompany one another as back and front follow one another.

16. The *Tao Te Ching* is a Chinese classic text credited to 6th century BCE sage Lao Tzu.

So this is the world in which we live. Within this world there are a number of resonances and reflections and echoes that are important for our understanding, because it is through these things that we can situate our experience. Memory is one of them. If we didn't have memories—if we couldn't remember things for a few minutes, or a few seconds, even—we wouldn't know that we existed. So we do what we can to enhance our memory: We remember what we can; we write things down; we make recordings; we take pictures.

Many of us have experiences that resemble the following scenario:

> We are having a wonderful or remarkable time with family and friends and someone says:
>
> *Oh, has anyone got a camera, so we can capture this special moment? In the months and years to come we will want to recall all the marvelous things that happened today.*
>
> Someone else might counter by saying:
>
> *No, no no, that's completely false! There isn't any other time than right now. There's only the single moment in which we all exist. There isn't any past. There isn't any future. Those are all illusions.*
>
> And a third friend might chime in with:
>
> *No! God has placed us in the world so that we might have experiences of the world. We are in this perfect laboratory, classroom, so that we can learn from our experiences. Otherwise we wouldn't be here.*

Then others of our group might air their views:

No, that's all nonsense! As soon as you step behind the lens of that camera you take yourself out of that experience.

So what's to be done here?

We know that we live in the world. And we know that God has put us here. And we have confidence that He has done so for a good reason. On the other hand, we know that the world is a ravening wolf, and that the world will destroy us. It will disperse us. It will entertain us and occupy us until all of our time is gone.

Because of this we seek refuge in our hearts, in the interior life, and we long for a retreat, an opportunity to step out of the world and concentrate on what's important. Yet on the other hand, we must live in the world.

So which of these philosophies is right? Well, as you probably know, both are right. We are called to be in the world but not of the world. It is our duty to invoke God in our hearts *and* learn from this perfect classroom in which He has placed us so that we can learn about ourselves, so that we might come to know Him.

So how is it that we are to do both things? Well, it's very simple. When you find yourselves overwhelmed or distracted or dispersed, or crushed by your life in the world, then it's time to retreat, to get your bearings again, to remember who you are, to find yourself at peace. But when you are centered and safe again, then you must go back into the world, because God has placed us in the world, and there are lessons there that we must learn.

In Zen, this is what's called "bringing the bull back to town."[17] We go to the forest in retreat to find the bull, and then

17. *The Ten Oxherding Pictures*:www.tricycle.org/magazine/ten-oxherding-pictures. Martine Batchelor. [online, accessed 20 December 2020]

we tame it. But having done that, then we need to take the bull back to town, because that's where life is. And the goal of the spiritual life is to bring these two things together, so that we can take the knowledge that we find in retreat, and bring that to an experience in the world, so that we can see the world in God. This is sometimes called walking on the razor's edge. But this is also called the path.

The Critique of Modernity

Intellectuals in general and Traditionalists[18] in particular encounter a special temptation to distance themselves from the world. This temptation is an occupational hazard of the true call of Traditionalism, for Traditionalists have a special vocation to the times in which we live. Analyzing and exposing the errors of the world around us has a place in this calling. A gardener must be able to tell the difference between a weed and a vegetable before the garden may be tended. Errors must be identified before they can be contrasted with corresponding truths, especially errors that are so much a part of a cultural consciousness that people do not even realize that they hold them.

Similarly, it would be a mistake to believe that the errors that surround us have had no influence on our own understanding of God and the world: No matter how explicitly we reject them, we may find that they still infect our perception. By understanding the false principles that ground the doctrines of modernity, we may hope more thoroughly to purge their effects on us.

18. The designations "Traditionalist" and "Perennialist" are nearly synonymous and are, for all intents and purposes, interchangeable. All of the major 20th-century writers in this area wrote of tradition. By this they meant the entirety of the intellectual, religious, cultural, and artistic aspects that tie a people to a revelation or to a sacred origin. Thus, the tradition is itself considered sacred. All things centered on this tradition, such as a civilization, its arts or crafts, its doctrines, etc., can be referred to as "traditional."

Every religious tradition understands the vocation of the prophet who is commissioned by God to deliver a call of repentance to His people. In order to repent, we must first recognize our sin. Here we may think not only of the prophets of the Hebrew scriptures, but of those whose vocation it is to demand change in the world. We may say, then, that both those who embrace Tradition and those who reject it can be proper audiences for a Traditionalist critique of the modern world.

There is a place for exposing the insidious errors of modernism so that someone who embraces Tradition may root out the false assumptions of modernism, and there are many examples in Perennialist literature of this project. But it is fair to ask if all, or even most, of Traditionalist criticism of modernity is placed at the service of these projects of purification and instruction? When Perennialists engage in the critique of the modern world among themselves, either in informal conversation, in a lecture at a conference, or in a published article, are they usually critiquing modernism for these purposes?

If not, what is the purpose of the critique—and what is its effect? Does it inspire listeners and readers to bring the light of Tradition to those who need it so badly—or does it inspire them to simply separate themselves all the more from the world? Does it always cause them to examine their own failure to embrace or fully understand Tradition, or does it sometimes only breed complacency—*I thank you Lord that I am not like them?*

It is a spiritual error—and indeed an error in anyone's daily life—to take your identity from that which you oppose. Of course, we must all avoid or oppose a specific manifestation of evil when called upon to do so. Yet to be preoccupied with evil, or an evil, is to build a bridge to it and to give it residence in your mind and soul. This is one of the prominent errors of the modern world: Most people can tell you what they are against, but have a great deal of difficulty telling you what they stand for. It is one thing to understand the errors of modernism; it is another thing to take your identity from opposing them.

There are three problems with defining your belief according to what you oppose. The first is the problem of identifying yourself with something negative. The second is that spotting and cataloging the errors of others and the world produces a false elitism, as if knowing the errors of the other automatically makes you a better person. It is a subtle trap. But third, even more subtle, is that in making pronouncements about the world, you tend to see the world as something separate from yourself. It is "outside." It is the "other." Certainly there are errors in the world and in ourselves (and the microcosm always reflects the macrocosm), but God is here, too.

It is similar to talking about sacred places. People are often encouraged to go to holy places to deepen or recharge their spiritual lives. Yes, yes, yes, there is something about Lourdes, the Black Hills, Delphi, Medjugorje. Yes, true. But there isn't anything there that isn't here; right here, right now.

For the sake of our own spiritual path, then, we must guard against contempt for the modern world. Criticism of modernity as an end in itself produces a feeling of self-satisfaction whose only effect is to damage those who engage in it. It creates a chimerical spirituality based not on the truth itself, but rather on our possession of the truth. This subtle shift in focus produces a kind of elitism, supported not even by knowledge of the truth, but by the identification of errors in others. This elitism feeds us with a false sense of transcendence. If we begin to think of evil as "out there," or below us, we are distracted from the evil within ourselves. The identification of the error in others becomes an unwitting detour for those who started out searching for a spiritual path.

A False Understanding of Evil in the World

All people who believe in God face evil and suffering in their own lives and struggle to understand it in light of what they know of God's goodness and mercy. For example, people speak of a painful event as a "blessing in disguise," and sometimes even assume that there must be such a blessing in all suffering, even if it's not visible yet. But the very phrase—"a blessing in disguise"—is ridiculous in terms of understanding reality, because the phrase defines "good" solely in terms of what benefits the suffering person personally on the corporeal or secular level, such as when an unpleasant event has a positive result. Already, the spiritual meaning or possibilities in life are lost.

Again, people speak of "putting yourself in the Hands of God." Understood in its shallowest form, this phrase sets up an absurd and impossible sort of fantasy of passivity with respect to your soul. The unspoken idea behind the phrase is that "everything will work out for the best." Again, the emphasis is on what is best on the merely secular level.

Does God interfere in human affairs at all? The question is wrong-headed from the outset. Those who believe in God tend to separate all events into two categories: those subject to the laws of nature and what we might call providential coincidences, when God decides to take a break from His usual routine of leaving earthly things alone, and pull some strings down here in the world. The effect of this false dichotomy is to rob us of the spiritual habit of extracting meaning from *every* moment.

"I do not think," says the typical theist, "that God always interferes discretely in human affairs. If humankind were to jump into the Grand Canyon one by one, we would all most assuredly hit the bottom." This is a perfectly illogical sentence. The phrase "interferes discretely" is a Newtonian phrase. What it almost always means in people's minds is an event that defies the laws of nature—something like, "I've never seen a rock fall skyward. If I did, that would be evidence of the existence of God." But Newtonian laws (and all such laws) are mathematical, abstract descriptions of phenomena. To science's consternation, quantum-level phenomena do not obey New-ton's laws. In fact, quanta are acknowledged to communicate instantaneously (a poor word, because there is no instant) across vast distances, and also blink in and out of existence (that is, corporeality).

But there is a more important flaw in such thinking: When the mental view is limited to matter and time, it causes people to overlook or deny those moments of wonder in which the world becomes, for an instant, transparent. How would you classify such a moment? Is it an instance of God "interfering discretely" in your human affairs? The solution to the whole conundrum is to keep sight of both the transcendence and the immanence of God.

Natural Disasters: The Problem of Evil

There have been a number of questions lately about the various disasters in the world: earthquakes in Haiti, Chile, and Turkey and the Tsunami in the Pacific and in the Indian Ocean some years ago. And there have been questions about what these things mean. Some say that these things are a Divine punish-ment for people or cultures who have become decadent or devi-ant. Others say no, this is a Divine mercy, and a way of taking people who are essentially innocent out of the world before they can be corrupted by the forces of modernism.

That's all conjecture. There is, however, a deeper meaning that's more immediate and more important to all of us, and it is this: When you hear about these events, in a mysterious way they become included in your own experience. Then, somehow, you have to embed them within your own experience in a similarly mysterious way. To do that, you must put yourself in the context of the situation: Imagine yourself on the streets of Turkey or Chile with the ground shaking and the buildings falling down around you. Imagine yourself on a beach in Phuket or Sri Lanka with a wave a mile long and 600 feet high about to crash down on you.

And what is it that you say in that moment? Do you say, "Get me out of here"? Do you say, "Lord, if You'll save me, I'll be good, I'll be better, I'll invoke more"? Do you say, "Lord, you can't take me now. I have too much important work to do. I have a family to support. I have children to educate. I have important things I must accomplish"? What is it *you* say?

That question rapidly morphs into a much more important question, which is: *Are you prepared to die right now? Not at some undefined point in the future. Not when you're old and tired and ready. But right now.* Because there are no guarantees that the sun's going to rise tomorrow, or that if it does, any of us are going to be here to see it. So when you ask the question: *What do these things mean?*, the meaning is very clear: It's a trial, and it's a test. And it's a trial and a test for you personally.

Aesthetics and Decoration in Our Life

I'm here to talk about aesthetics, art and decoration and how these things are applied practically at the level of our homes and our lives. I am not here to talk about the philosophy and metaphysics of aesthetics and beauty—there are others who are more qualified than I—but to share how we can integrate our spirituality and our daily life on the path.

Everything we do is done with a view toward the invocation of God and the interior life. And all the elements of our lives, including the places we live and the things we surround ourselves with, have a role to play in our interiority and in our invocation of God. Nothing is there by accident, and much is to be gained by doing everything we can as individual beings to try to facilitate our own interior lives.

In classical times, both in the classical Greek period and in the Middle East, when people designed a city, one of the requirements of the design was that the city would be responsible for making the people who lived there better people. The layout of the city, the design of the buildings, the geometries that were involved, the proportions that people ran into every day—these things would make people better. These material things would lead toward better individuals and hence a better society. That's been pretty much lost, although you can get a glimpse of it by realizing that 21st-century people spend vast sums of money going to visit these places that were designed so; but nobody spends a lot of money to visit a shopping center for the sake of its architecture.

All of this has to do with something that we generally call aesthetics, and although that term has come to mean taste and beauty and good looks, the root of the word had a much different sense. The term in Greek has to do with perception. It has to do with keeping the gates of perception open. I've tracked this word all the way back to its Indo-European root, and it means the same thing. Aesthetics has to do with making the senses open so that you can see and feel and touch and taste the higher harmonies of the world. You do so by this aesthetic, which is intended to facilitate that.

The use of proportion and color and line are very important in preserving a kind of harmony and openness that we want to facilitate in our lives and in our homes.

In terms of the use of aesthetics in our lives, there are really three principal areas.

The most important is our sacred space. We should have a particular look and plan for our sacred space. The sacred space is the one part of your house that is purely hallowed, and it is important that the things there really should be sacred items and forms and designs and art. Since the sacred space is a special place, it's necessary to screen it off from the rest of the house or living area.

Within the house or apartment again, we should decorate in such a way that is calm, that lifts us up, that calls us to the interior and raises us up to Heaven. We're drawn to simplicity, to ease, to rest, because what we're really doing is facilitating our own interiority.

We want our clothing to be an expression of the world that we want to fit into, so that it will not disturb us as we conduct our lives nor draw attention to ourselves by inappropriate gaudiness.

Sacred Space Within Your Main House/Apartment

* Keep it simple
* Screened off from the main living space
* Blinds/curtains to windows
* Decorations: verse from sacred text/traditional items
* Avoid extremes

LIVING SPACE: HOUSE/APARTMENT

* Keep it simple
* Unostentatious
* Mostly solid colors
* Decorations uncluttered
* Small number of sacred objects
* Rotate individual items if you have many
* Furniture: clean lines—think Swedish modern
* Color, design appropriate to context/culture/climate
* Avoid extremes

CLOTHING

* Keep it simple
* Unostentatious
* Colors and patterns appropriate to context, culture and climate
* NOT an expression of ego
* NOT gaudy
* Avoid extremes

For ease of reference, on the previous page I've set out the principles and some details of how to incorporate these aesthetics into our lives. So these things are said in a particular context. But above all, the principle is that the design, the environment, the ambience, should draw us to the interior, because there is a relationship between the ambiance and the effect it will have on the soul.

The outward really does have an effect on the interior. And if I could reduce this to a couple of words, it would be "avoid extremes." Avoid all extremes in this area. As much as we like beautiful things, we don't want to have too many of them. And as much as we want to dress or live in simple stasis, we don't want that to be too extreme either. These things get to be more complicated the more one lives in this world. But those are the principles.

Question: *Can you please elaborate on how you define the term "activism"?*

Response: We should all try to make the best choices with respect to our fellow humans, our animal companions, and the world we live in. That is required and is a part of spiritual virtue, which is a constituent element of the spiritual life. Further, self-effacing acts such as serving others can have a softening effect on the egoistic shell that separates us from higher worlds. Moreover, as God's vicegerents on earth, we are enjoined to care for the world in which we live. Spiritually speaking, our involvement in the world—even in good works—takes our attention and distracts us from our awareness of the presence of the Divine. This can be a kind of trap, as it always seems easier to "do something" than it is to be detached and to pray/meditate/invoke. Certainly, we should all do good works, but with the understanding that the best work we can ever do—for ourselves and for the world we live in—is interior prayer and the remembrance of God's holy

Name. All other human acts pale in comparison.

I am reminded of two things here. First is the story from the Ramayana, the epic Hindu scripture in which Rama has created a magic bubble to protect Sita, his wife, during his absence. The forces of evil try to approach Sita but are always rebuffed by the magic bubble. Finally, the demon presents itself as an old man in need of assistance, and Sita leaves the protection of the bubble to aid him. The demon seizes her, and disaster and war follow. That bubble, for us, is the spiritual life, and its quintessential act is the remembrance of God. Be wary of worthy causes—not that they are unworthy, but as Jesus said, "Seek ye first the kingdom of heaven." (Matthew 6:33). The biblical story of Mary and Martha (Luke 10:38-42) makes the same point.

The second thing that comes to mind is a personal story. Some time ago I was talking with a student who was working on a degree in English literature. He was studying the work of the poet William Blake at that point, so I asked, "What is Blake's work about?" He replied, "Social justice." So, I asked, "What is Wordsworth about?" He replied, "Social justice." "And Coleridge?" I asked. His reply was—you guessed it—"social justice."

This describes the current cultural moment and the phase in the cosmic cycle in which we live. This is not to say that social injustice is a new phenomenon, or that history and ancient times could not have benefited from a greater social consciousness. By no means. But that is not the cultural emphasis of current times. This emphasis on social justice began in the Renaissance[19] as the worldview changed its focus from God to man. This has continued apace with modern philosophies, perhaps Karl Marx and Thomas Paine being the most obvious. In any event, this is part and parcel of the modernist fantasy. So, yes, do good works as you can, but try to save your energy and attention for the protection and development of your interior life, your invocation, and your practice of the awareness of the Divine.

19. 14th – 17th Century CE in Europe.

Question: *Why do bad things happen, and why is there injustice in the world?*

Response: You asked a serious question and I want to give you a considered response. There are misguided efforts to make these "bad things" acceptable by changing the nature of God or by saying that there are "mysteries." That term, "mysteries," is actually incorrect in this context. Properly, the term "mysteries" is not used to describe something that cannot be understood; rather it is used to describe something that can't be expressed. Language is really very limited in its ability to describe profound realities.

But as you are interested in this topic, I thought I would try to explain it from a point of view that is purely metaphysical, which, I suspect, will be more satisfying to you than trying to say what God does and doesn't know. The problem is ancient, and it is known as "the problem of evil." So, from the point of view of pure metaphysics, here is an explanation of what evil is and how it works.

God creates the world. But to say "creation" is to say a kind of otherness and distance. Of course, nothing can ever be distant from or other than God. Yet created things are relatively less God than pure God Himself (otherwise they would still be part of Pure Him, and not created). Most wisdom traditions try to describe this with various analogies and personifications. In Christianity, the best description is probably from Meister Eckhart, who differentiates God (and all things are God) from the Godhead (which is purely Him and beyond being and existence). Good so far?

So, God creates things and they exist (the etymology of the word "exist" is accurate in the metaphysical sense of *ex*, "out or forth," and *sistere*, "to stand"). Now, the things that exist are no longer purely part of the Godhead. So we can talk about a distance between pure God and created things. This distance is often described as a kind of movement away from the Divine

98

creative Principle that sets it in motion. However, since God is the source of being, this movement away from God is ultimately in the direction of non-being or, almost paradoxically, of non-existence.

Some wisdom traditions describe existence as things radiating from a Divine Center and some describe things descending from a Divine Perfection. But, in any case, there is a kind of separation and distance that, necessarily, accompanies the process of creation or manifestation. Without this distance or projection, God would be entirely in Himself, and there would be no creation, no manifested world, no us.

Since God is Good, the direction of this movement, or projection, away from God is sometimes called "evil." From this point of view, evil does not have a reality of its own, but only exists as a direction into which creation is deployed. Evil is necessarily a consequence of creation, which is a separation from God. The evil we see around us—the pain, injustice and suffering—is part and parcel of this separation. This is true of all creation as, clearly, these things do not exist in God, the Godhead.

Of course, it must also be said that all that exists never loses its connection to God, or to the Center; nevertheless, manifestation, by its very nature, implies a distance—but not a separation—from the Principle. This distance—or separation or descent—from God is the ontological basis of evil.

But all this is metaphysical speculation, which varies from one system to another. Such speculation inevitably exposes the paradoxical nature of applying our human reasoning and human systems to the vast multiplex perfection that is the eternal Principle manifesting as our phenomenal world. Certainly, the reality is the same, but the expressions can be increasingly difficult to compare. Moreover, regardless of the language we use, whether English or Latin or Sanskrit or mathematics or poetry or music, we must understand that all these attempts to express the truth are at the very limit of the expressible. That's why they are sometimes called "mysteries."

So, evil has no real existence of its own, but it appears in our world, and we must deal with the error, pain, and suffering that manifest it. But, finally, nothing that is can ever be separated from God. In this understanding, I find the basis for both peace and faith and some facility to deal with the evil I encounter. This is life.

It is only normal to want justice at our level of experience, but that is not always possible, and, more important, the world of phenomena is incredibly subtle and complex. Yet we know that there is a final Divine Justice; we know that ultimately the good wins (because it is more real than that which opposes it); but we also have to have the faith to leave the details to God. It is easy in the spiritual life to be distracted by efforts to do good and noble things in the world we see around us. This is not to say that we should not do what we can if and when we have the opportunity. Nevertheless, the most important act we can accomplish on earth—for the good of all—is to maintain our interior prayer. Nothing in life is more important. Nothing we can do will benefit the world more. Moreover, we can make this choice at every moment.

Our response to phenomena and experience can be intense and emotional. That is part of our makeup, also given by God. But it is essential that we not be carried away by these things, even when they are close and poignant. Let me suggest to you that there is a higher attitude: acceptance of the world as it is, with all its "flaws," and deep sorrow for those involved, not just the innocents, but the perpetrators, too, as they are blind and hard and broken and deeply lost. Then turn from the world and back to God to affirm the Eternal Good. The world is a place of darkness and light, of certainty and mystery, of good and bad, of complexities and contradictions.

Question: *The descent of time, the thickening of the cosmos so that* *it no longer manifests God as clearly as it once did, must be part of God's design for creation (manifestation). And if it is, how can it be evil?*

Response: The condemnation of the "reign of quantity"[20] is not for those who live within it to make; it is for the chosen few who exist apart from it—those who live in this age, but are actually part of another age. This is the Perennialist perspective. We can only see the "reign of quantity" (or, for that matter, any other phenomenon) by stepping out of it. We may condemn its errors precisely to the extent that we stand apart from it and thus can see them.

But it is one thing to condemn its errors, and it is another thing to condemn its existence. The claim that some towering figures are not part of the current age seems very dangerous to me, as it amounts to rejecting the very classroom into which God has put us. He has chosen this time and place for us to come to know Him. But even without this danger, your point stands: The descent of time—the thickening of the cosmos so that it no longer manifests God as clearly as it once did—must be part of God's design for creation (manifestation). And if it is, how can it be evil?

The real question is: What does this mean to us? How shall we then live? The belief that the cosmos is thickening implies that the reality in which God has placed us is a world of flow and flux. And, finding ourselves in it, we must make choices about how we are going to live. Our choice can be to attach ourselves to that which is most holy and has the firmest connection to the Source in order that we might use that connection to regain the lost paradise where we can reclaim our true selves.

20. *The Reign of Quantity and the Signs of the Times* is a 1945 book by the French intellectual René Guénon, in which the author purports to give a comprehensive explanation, based on tradition, of the cyclical conditions that led to the state of the modern world in general and to the Second World War in particular.

Evil is that which leads us away or fixes us in place or, worse yet, persuades us that this Divine drama is not really at play. These things should be of critical interest to us, as the truth and our True Home is with God in the center. Those things that dazzle, distract, and mollify us in order that we do not oppose the flow outward or downward from the center we may see as "evil." In our world these errors are intellectual and moral, and it is religion (*religare*: to bind fast) that provides the direction and the means back to the Center.

So, on Saturday afternoon you encounter evil. Perhaps it stands before you as an example of greed or cruelty, or perhaps it stands inside you as an example of pride or lust. For example, a hypothetical person says: "All is one, all is God, therefore nothing that is of God can be harmed in its essence, so I may do as I please in (for instance) operating a pyramid scheme that deprives hundreds of a decent pension and all their savings."

These things in their relative existence need to be opposed and expunged. A clear evil, even though it has legitimate metaphysical roots, must be opposed and expunged. This is the battle we are here to fight. We can only fight it for ourselves, but that is just what we must do. To do less is to allow ourselves to drown, on the grounds that God has created water and the flood has been willed by Him.

Chapter 9
On Transformation of the Self

Knowledge of the Self

THE KEY QUESTION IS NOT, WHAT'S TRUE? BUT, *Who am I?* This is not entirely an intellectual matter, for we are more than brains and minds. We have minds, according to the Quran,[21] so that we may know. Now, this particular kind of knowledge has nothing to do with acquiring data, as if the Day of Judgment were some kind of examination on principles or doctrine. The kind of knowledge here has nothing to do with information; it has to do with our own knowledge of ourselves and what we do with it. For, as the Prophet said, "He who knows himself, knows his Lord."[22] We do not become holy or realized by "figuring it out"; we become holy by transforming ourselves. The mind has much to do with this process, as it is the facility that allows us to pay attention so that we may see. But seeing is not enough; we must do. We must practice that which we know.

Corporeality

There is an almost overpowering tendency among those who are bright and educated to think that they can figure it all out and grasp the sea of transcendent truth in their fingers. Just a little more learning... just the right angle of vision... the words from just the right sage... But that is false.

There is no final exam that will get you into Paradise. Being

21. "[This is] a blessed Book which We have revealed to you, [O Muhammad], that they might reflect upon its verses and that those of understanding would be reminded." Quran 38:29
22. Futûhât al-Makkiyyah 308.22

103

"right" about the world and existence is not enough. It may not be worth anything. There is an old Zen saying that enlightenment is not what you think. The only thing that is really at issue, ever, is your knowledge of yourself. Your life and the world you are in have been created for this sole purpose. Not so you can "get it right" but so that you can "know who you are." Nothing else matters. You can't find it in books. You can't find it in the world, although it is always there staring you in the eyes.

There is a panoply of things that are here to help you: religion, doctrine, action, prayer. The only work that really matters is the work of transforming yourself—not so you can know, but so you can be that which knows. But you must start with the small things, the little actions, the little realizations that come as almost indistinguishable points of light that illuminate your soul and make you feel higher, more at peace, and closer to the Divine. It is the only work that matters at all, but it will cost you all of your attachments to your view of reality and the positions you hold so strongly. But there is nothing else to do. It is the only thing that matters. It is worth all your effort. It is worth everything. Are you ready to start?

Corporeality is a mirror for the self. We must understand and see ourselves in every encounter with corporeality. Every accusation that is made against the "other" is an accusation that is equally valid for ourselves, for the quality of the accused is also an indisputable element of our own soul. For example, if we accuse the world of injustice, we must confront the fact that not only have we practiced injustice, but that both the capacity to do so and the actualizing of that element have occurred numerous times. And we must know that this is true of ourselves.

For those who cannot interrogate themselves, the very accusation against the other is nothing other than an ego-claim that one is different from that other. When a person says: "I would love more, or better, if I received more from the other," he or she is hiding and failing to recognize *themselves* as a constructor of conditions that allow them to withdraw love. Under this paradigm, unhappiness is always the fault of the other. To think that you are an objective, disinterested observer can place you in a position in which you will always and forever consider yourself an exception to whatever you disapprove of.

That is not the way. The essence of esotericism is not about framing a hypothesis such as your hypothesis that "unity with others is, in effect, the by-product of unity with God." That is a philosophical hypothesis that is at odds with the essence of esotericism. But more importantly, the question is: *How do I execute the experiment?* If you pose such a hypothesis, what can I say? There is no discussion of such a hypothesis that will lead you to its test, unless you would expect someone to tell you how to attain unity with God so that you become one with others.

Divine Awareness

World, life, ego: In the center is the supreme Name that nothing can withstand. This notion of center, of the still point through which we must pass as spiritual travelers, is everywhere in mysticism. It is the eye of the needle. It is the gateless gate. It is the neck of the hourglass. It is everywhere. Now, this is beautiful language, and it is so easy to see this as simply a metaphor or as symbol or as poetry. And it is all of those things. There is a quality of the mind that makes it impossible to focus or think about or concentrate on more than one thing at a time. Certainly, we think we think about more than one thing at a time; but we really don't. Consequently, if we fill our mind and our attention and our awareness with the Divine Name, we necessarily exclude the world, and necessarily exclude the ego. This is a victory.

Many schools of Buddhism, including Zen, assert: "Just to meditate is to reach Nirvana." In the Gospels, Jesus says: "Be of good cheer: I have overcome the world." [John 16:33] This is that victory. When we fill our attention and our awareness with the Divine Name, we overcome the world, and we overcome our ego. This is our mission. This is why we were born. This is our victory. And of course, it is God's victory. But it is available constantly: every time you pray, every time you invoke the Divine Name. If you are present and if you fill your awareness with the Supreme Name, you will necessarily overcome the ego and the world. This is always available. We tend to think things are complicated, but nothing could be simpler.

On Love

Love is not a matter of metaphysical understanding. That may appeal to the intellect, but it doesn't really have anything to do with the substance of love. Neither does objective truth for that matter, as love has the unique property of remaining truly what it is even though its object be undeserving.

Love is not to be understood and then practiced. It is to be practiced so that it may be understood. That understanding is an understanding of ourselves, for the practice of love—if we pay attention—is a powerful opportunity to observe and manage manifold aspects of ourselves and to observe and remove the dross that blinds us and makes us smaller. Love is an essential part of the spiritual path of self-knowledge and enlightenment. Love is not a thing to be seen and observed; it is thing to be done and perfected.

Divine Love should not be thought of as a state of being. A state of being implies other states. Divine Love is not a state. Corporeal love, where known, is a state of knowing the Real. Unity with others is not a by-product of unity with God. In truth, there is no such thing as unity with others in the sense of some sort of generalized mental benevolence. The key with respect to others is acceptance of their necessity as a means of knowing yourself, and thus knowing God.

This work is the occupation of the inner man, the essence of esotericism. We never automatically become anything, and certainly not one with others. One must know *oneself* in others. Corporeal love must not be thought of as a "thing" in the abstract or as affected by corporeal conditions. At the level of corporeal life, this is the very error that causes people to falsely assume that if everything were to their liking, they would somehow know how to love. People will say, for example, "I love my children." This is untrue. What they really mean is "I love my children when they don't oppose me or disappoint me or refuse to do as I wish. I love them too because they are mine and not those of some stranger." Most people do not love their spouses, because they have formulated a long list of reasons why their spouse deserves less love. They do not understand that the value of love lies in loving without expectation, for its own sake. This is the love that changes the soul.

Seeing Ourselves in the Other

You and I will die, and the world will continue on. It is perfectly illogical to die in a state of bitterness or despair regarding the idiocy of the world. What value does this have? Would it be a consolation to draw our last breath to say: "I was right?" Would it be satisfying to be given a large trophy engraved with all of the times and dates on which it was asserted that some "idiocy" had taken place, a trophy that would be a record of all the times one was right? There are those who go to their deaths in exactly this manner, recounting every slight, every time they were short-changed by people or the world, and hugging their resentment to their breasts, bitter that they now must die, when they feel they shouldn't be required to do so because they were so much righter than anyone else.

Judgment of the world is not your job. If anything, you might be moved to pray for people to awaken, or simply say: "Go with

God" silently to them; for they choose their own fates, and they live with their own states. And if someone cheats you, of course you can try to recover that loss, but you and only you make the decision for yourself as to whether you will cheat. You can possess the knowledge of yourself that is honest and true: that you fully possess the capacity to cheat, and have done so in your own life. This will help you avoid feeling superior to others.

And you can, with this knowledge of yourself, know the difference in the effects upon your own soul of cheating or not cheating if you use your mind for its intended purpose, which is to inform the soul that the inner content of cheating is a felt kind of lowness and "grayness"; and the content of not cheating is higher and clearer. And that the former makes no logical sense to cling to, for its effects are perfectly useless in terms of clarity and peace; while the latter possesses traces of inner light. We choose what we will be. We feel sorry for the cheater. The judgment is not yours; it is God's. Divine Love is radiated incessantly. God roots for the cheater to find those higher states, and He also roots for you. And when you can effect these transformations within yourself, you can no longer hate the cheater. You can no longer feel superior.

So it is not in the metaphysical realm that you learn, but in the small moments of ordinary life. You must see yourself in the other; for you have all the same capacities as whoever or whatever you are accusing. You are never superior or higher. You merely know more and you are merely beginning, in small increments, to shed whatever has no spiritual usefulness within *yourself*. Pay no attention to anyone who remains mired in the corporeal illusion of thinking the world is fundamentally purposeless, and exists solely for satisfying their own desires to get or dominate or be "successful" (or right). For such a one, death comes as a bitter end, for none of these "accomplishments" can be held onto. All of their putative value is extinguished by death.

But the complex and sometimes excruciating process of truly knowing yourself—objectively and without totaling up good points and bad points—and then shedding whatever is spiritually useless—this yields tranquility. For if you keep choosing the higher over the lower, and if you stay focused on the small things in actions and reactions, you will see that indeed the world is perfect for its intended purpose. It will have been that very world that provided the opportunities for you to learn and know what is real. There is no other place. There is no other time. This life is where you learn (or not) to know God. And if you do, you will know that if you were God, you would have created the world exactly as it is, for there is no other place than this corporeal classroom in which you can be both subject and object of scrutiny.

With respect to love, it isn't that Divine Love manifests Itself when you acquire Godly perfection. Divine Love manifests when you know that you can never be perfect, yet you choose to abandon conditional love and decide to learn what it is to love unconditionally (even a single other human, for this learning must take place in the corporeal realm). In human experience, such an experiment reveals a force indescribably powerful and pure, a giving that is done *for its own sake*, not for any sort of getting. And this knowledge, in turn, brings a far stronger and far more powerful force into your awareness, leaving no doubt whatsoever as to that Reality's reality.

When you are counting the people in the world who truly understand, you don't unthinkingly include yourself in that number. If you do not understand yourself, then the you that you wish others to understand is very likely a dramatic fiction of your own creation—a secret self that somehow seems to be the real self. I assure you that your real self is most probably the one you don't know. It further suggests that you have framed a condition by which you judge others, such as the requirement that they understand you, while exonerating yourself from any obligation to understand them. This puts you in a position of being the judge, jury, and executioner for all others. Is this a warm, happy, or in some way transcendent state to be in? Does it give you peace?

I sense that your inner landscape seems fairly bleak. Perhaps it is this that is causing you to see the outer world as hopelessly flawed. To feel totally isolated is a state that can be unbearable. The remedy is to refuse to live in that state—to make a conscious decision that you will do anything to get to a better place, because you see that the alternative is self-destruction. The remedy is to re-direct your attention to very small things—to find meaning and perception not from philosophy or metaphysics, but right in front of you, and to do this every day.

I would suggest that you find an anthill and spend an hour or more sitting cross-legged and watching its activities, until you have rid your mind of what it thinks it knows about ants, and simply begins to address what is really before it, which is a mystery. The next day, do the same by pulling a weed up by the roots and spending an hour contemplating it as it actually is, which is also a great mystery. Think about the fact that you, by pulling it up by its roots, have killed it. Make no judgments about whether that was a bad act or a good act.

The next day, sit quietly in a place where you will not be distracted, and close your eyes for an hour. In your mind, visualize yourself as just your skeleton—no flesh, no organs. Put your fingers on your jaw bone and open and close your mouth. When you move your arm, see your bones move in your mind. Be aware that you are an animated skeleton. Again, rid your mind of what it "knows" about muscles and blood and all other explanations, until you can see the mystery and can no longer understand how an animated skeleton can possibly move, let alone think. Now allow that skeleton to pray. Experience amazement. Experience wonder. Experience beauty. Experience the miraculous. Forget metaphysics for those three days.

Question: *How is the Self different from ego?*

Response: Distinguishing between the ego and the Self is not like a play in which the ego is a separate character (the villain) and the Self a wonderful character off-stage whom you can't see but know is the hero. This is to have a mental caricature of what you are. To know yourself is not complete; nor does it constitute understanding to think that to know yourself is to know your villain. This is because it pits you against yourself. To view the ego from the perspective of the Self is a process that leaves the villain completely as it was—a permanent resident on the stage. You cannot make a distinction between the ego as independent from both you and Self, because you and ego are not two separate characters; they are the same character. You do not cease identifying with the ego; you prune it; you eliminate things that are useless from it; and when you do so, small rays of light have room to manifest themselves. As long as you are locked in the conflict between you and your ego, you are stuck and you give the ego more reality than it deserves.

Many people pit themselves against the villain as though there is a third character, namely themselves, who is going to defeat the villain and by doing so get to know the hero. And so a little play is enacted in the mind. But you do not have to know who you are to say that you are the villain. This pits you against yourself. There is no possibility of defeating this villain, because the villain remains a permanent resident on the stage. Some assume that if they could ever defeat the villain, the hero would magically appear. This presumes, also, that the hero is a separate character. The laughter of Maya (illusion) is heard behind the scenes.

Question: *How does one transform oneself?*

Response: The game is to actually bring out the other parts of the self (what you call "ego"), which transform the self into a character that has shed habits and behavior and thoughts, and shed them permanently, which allows what you call the Self to take over (or shine through or appear). This is what is called a station. It is not and cannot be an all-at-once transformation. It is, in fact, driven by the lower self. It is that lower self that makes the decisions. It is that self that is the rational mind. It is that very self that is capable of recognizing, dissecting, and deciding what it will no longer cling to because the things it is clinging to have no utility for it.

Transformation of the self is the cause; intellection is the effect. We do not transform the self through intellection. Intellection comes as a result of transformation of the self. The striving is not for intellection but for the recognition and acceptance and then shedding of one small non-useful practice and making room for a higher order of knowledge and awareness. In some ways this could be described as just as physical and mechanical as digging actual weeds out of actual dirt. It really is about the lower self being ruthlessly objective.

Question: *Is identification with the Self the same as transformation of the self?*

Response: Identifying with the Self is not the same as transformation of the self. We must work with our actual "clay," not with a constant effort at comparison. It is a process for making room for the Self, not identifying with it. That is not different from identifying with the "hero," yet not knowing or finding out how to know or become the hero.

This is why I don't like the word "ego" to define the lower self. The lower self is inclusive of everything you are; one of the things you are is a thinking creature, not just a villain. It is that very mind that is capable of looking at itself, at you, with perfect objectivity and making perfectly rational decisions, perfectly logical decisions, to actually see what is useless to it. Once we see what is useless to us objectively (meaning, without rationalization, without excuses, without avoidance, and with acceptance), we can say to ourselves: *This has no positive utility to me, and I therefore will not do it any longer.*

To know one's self is to actually know one's self—not part of one's self, but all of one's self, every aspect of one's self. Can the self be ruthlessly objective toward itself? Of course it can. The proof of this is that many people actually do know themselves, and they don't like what they know. So they hide it—yet still cling to it, taking cold comfort in hating themselves or parts of themselves.

The self is perfectly capable of observing and analyzing itself. That is why God gives us a brain. "Identification with the ego" is a phrase that gives control to the ego. The self is then seen as victim, because the individual has a bifurcated view in which there are actually two selves locked in mortal combat. The ego is conflated with being powerful—much more powerful than it actually is. Ruthless objectivity, not in abstract terms but in very specific minute-by-minute terms, can provide the opportunity for self to ask self: *What exactly is the utility or the usefulness of this specific behavior or thought of mine?*

Here the self stops trying to defeat the villain, and, instead, brings the villain much closer—embraces the villain, in fact. And when we embrace the villain, we can address it as an object of the science of the soul and ask: *What exactly was that moment of blame, or that moment of pettiness, or that moment of resentment, really like? What did I feel? What useful effect did it have? Did it make me feel higher? Did it make me feel better? Did I feel a little ray of light enter me?*

And if the answer is no, the wonderful brain that God has provided us with is perfectly capable of logically and rationally and gently saying: *Why am I doing this? What benefit have I gained?* And if we can address oourselves without fear (which is precisely what causes war within us), we are perfectly capable of saying: *That's really absurd. I don't need it. It doesn't do one thing for me that feels good and I'm dropping it from my repertoire.* By bringing that "sin" closer and really examining it, the self can more quickly recognize that part of itself, when it shows up with an invitation to pettiness, rationalization, bitterness, or any number of behaviors and thoughts that in fact have no utility or usefulness whatever. And instead of trying to destroy the self, we can simply drop that behavior or thought because it is perfectly useless.

Be confident! This transformation is within your power. The self is the one who decides. The self is the one who examines objectively, and the self is the one who makes intelligent decisions based upon the efficacy of everything that touches the self's mind and heart—from the smallest self-deception to the smallest act of malice to the smallest interaction with the world that causes envy. All these can be recognized and brought closer for an examination of their nature and effects, and then shed from our behavior and thoughts.

But this is not done all at once, or by assertion or vow. It is done one occasion at a time by examining one interaction with the world at a time, and focusing just on that one case or event until we can see it as it really is—useless—and recognize it every time it shows up, until we can banish it from existence.

To "die before dying" does not mean ceasing to identify with the ego. This, too, implies that the ego is a separate character in the play. Who is it who is doing the ceasing? Is that yet a third character? It cannot be the Self, because the Self has no ego. It is the self who makes every decision; that self that has been given reflection by God as a partner for its mind. As for pain and suffering, if the self assumes that pain and suffering is the way to wrench the ego into the Self, why has the self failed to give equal power to the moments and mini-intellections of joy, peace, love, and happiness as being equally capable of wrenching the villain into the Self?

It is, in fact, the self that recognizes and seeks more of the

Light; and it is by this same recognition that the self knows what to shed. To say that we "have to expose our egos and our bodies to considerable pain and suffering" would imply that some "one" is making these decisions—another character in the play. Is it the villain (ego)? Is it the real self? Who would that be? In truth, the self makes none of these decisions. God plainly says: "I bring all of the good things that happen to you and all of the bad things—the trials—to you." The issue is: What does the self learn from them? To learn from them is the self's job.

In brief, all the characters are really one character: yourself, which includes every aspect of mind, emotion, body, soul, and humanness—and the capacity to refashion itself and clear out the useless within to make space for the Light to come in. All the characters must be known and understood—objectively, not angrily—which commences with recognition, in very small steps, and then leads to the changes that the self/Self (or "you") makes with thoughts and behaviors. The hero does not come out from behind the curtain. It is the villain who is transformed when we truly know ourselves and act upon that knowledge. When we know and recognize that which bestows nothing high upon us, it is perfectly logical and rational to abandon those habits and delusions. Then the Light enters.

You cannot identify with any part of your self. You *are* your self. To "identify" with an arbitrarily defined and highly stereotyped part of your self means that you are comparing something you consider to be a neutral and aspect-free self to something you consider to be other. Thus, the fictional neutral self is presumed to either be aligning with a bad self or a good self. This is impossible. There is no neutral self to do the identifying. That is why the first step in God's instructions is *know* yourself. In this, to know means to know without judgment, without applying the words "good" or "bad." It means accepting your self in its entirety as being true.

Question: *What do you mean by saying that "identification with the ego" is a phrase that gives control to the ego?*

Response: The ego is, by definition, other than our self. Because of this, that other is seen as an independent agent. As an independent agent, it is presumed to have control over something. That something can only be, in this mental construct, the neutral human-aspect-free self. And it is that self that is the victim of the ego/other.

This view leads to a common error of blaming the "other" for our state. And blaming the ego is none other than a way to get off the hook and absolve this innocent neutral self of both its responsibilities and its very existence. It is very common to blame others of all kinds for our spiritual state or unhappiness or lack of peace. People blame their jobs, their spouses, their children, their parents, modernity, and a thousand others for their condition. The ego is only one other among many.

This blaming is not productive in any way. It does not contribute to knowledge of self or to shedding that which drags the soul down, so that we can allow the soul to rise. It is undeniable that each person *has* an ego. It is a possession of our self. It can be one's friend. It can be trained. It can be useful. For example: What part of the self makes the decision to seek God? It cannot be the Self. It has to be the self, because it is this that wishes to ascend. When you say to your self, "I want to know God," the "I" that is speaking is the human creation of God Himself. Therefore, rather than thinking in terms of identification with this or that, it is better to think in terms of "I am," because that statement is inclusive of every aspect, including Self. And thinking in terms of "I am" allows for the acceptance and knowing of everything you are, as opposed to identifying with pieces or parts of your self on a judgmental, polarized basis.

Question: *Can you explain what you mean by subjecting the elements of our soul (or self) that we perceive as villainous to objective scrutiny?*

Response: Objective scrutiny is not limited to that which is villainous. It is, however, limited to our actual lived interactions with the world. For example, let's take a rather common situation that occurs in life, especially among parents:

Objective Scrutiny of the Self

Objective scrutiny can be applied to actual lived interactions with the world—for example, objective scrutiny of this small lived event. A parent says:

Statement	**My children don't call, my children don't write. I sent a gift and never got a thank-you.**
Ask yourself	What state am I in?
Answer	Annoyance. I am annoyed. Let me bring this annoyance much closer and see what it really is.
Ask yourself	Why am I annoyed?
Answer	I am annoyed because the "other" has failed me. This causes me to categorize the other negatively.
Ask yourself	Now, self, how does this make you feel?

(Pause for objective contemplation)

Objective Scrutiny of the Self (Cont.)

.../ Answer If I am honest with myself, it makes me feel superior to the other.

(Pause for more thought)

Ask yourself What utility does that have, oh self?
Does that make you feel happy?
Does that make you feel transcendent?
Does that give you peace?

(Pause for more thought)

Answer Well, no, it doesn't.

(Pause for small moment of astonishment.)

Ask yourself Then why are you thinking this, self?
Answer I don't know.
Ask yourself If you wanted to give a gift, why not just give it?
Why place conditions on your wish to give?
If you wanted to talk to your children, why didn't you call them?
If you wanted to write to them, why didn't you?
Why did you carefully formulate conditions for your generosity?
Why did you carefully formulate conditions for your love?
Tell yourself These conditions allowed you to be disappointed and annoyed.
Tell yourself You made the decisions, self, to be resentful.
Tell yourself You made the decisions to hold your children responsible for somehow "failing" you.

Objective Scrutiny of the Self *(Cont.)*

Here is an idea:

Ask yourself   Why don't you just drop that annoyance, that
expectation, that resentment?
If you never received a thank-you or a phone call
or a letter, how would that affect your decisions?
Why not give a gift, write a letter, or make a
phone call yourself?
Why not enjoy giving a gift, writing a letter or
making a phone call freely?
Why not enjoy the freedom of giving without
being tethered by conditions and expectations?

(Pause for small moment of realization)

Tell yourself   Well, self, I think you're right:
This pattern has no utility whatsoever in terms
of my state or improving it.
I will be much happier giving those gifts, calls,
and letters freely and without expectation,
I can just feel good doing it.
And now, self, we'll be able to recognize this
useless reaction the very next time we see it
in ourselves.
We will pay careful attention to recognizing it as
part of our self that has no utility whatsoever.
When I think that thought or say those words or
want to say them the next time, I will stop
and say:
"Go away. I will not entertain those thoughts
again."

What can be learnt from the preceding text:

Transformation is the result of what can only be called the "little things." It is the result of paying careful attention to your lived interaction with the world. And objectivity is to recognize and know yourself without judgment but with a clear eye toward what those interactions do for the soul in truth, and whether or not they drag the soul down or raise the soul up. Our ability to discern the difference between dragging ourselves down and allowing ourselves to rise is amazingly accurate. You will know instantly, if you pay attention to the actual moments of your lived experience, whether or not your behavior and thoughts have any benefit for your soul/self.

Pay close attention to what is happening when you laugh. It is a nanosecond of pure intellection.

Question: *I am trying to become the Perfect Man,[23] to be transformed. But no matter how sincerely I form the intention, I realize eventually that I have fallen back into my old ways.*

Response: There is no such thing as a sudden and complete transformation. It is a cumulative process of shedding that which has no utility, one small thing at a time, and learning to recognize it every time it rears its ugly head. I believe that perhaps the issue here is that you are not actually experiencing your ordinary life, which is, in fact, the real and the only path. You are trying to reach perfection in a single bound. No one reaches perfection in a single bound. Relax a little. Be a little

---

23. "Perfect Man" has a specific meaning in Muslim/Sufi practice and philosophy, particularly as discussed by the Sufi mystic scholar/poet, Ibn Arabi. As with many apparently complex concepts, the attainment of Perfection becomes simple, profound and all-embracing once concepts and words fall away and Reality shines throughout: ibnarabisociety.org/sufism-and-the-perfect-human.

kinder to yourself.

Question: *You say that to "die before you die" does not mean ceasing to identify with the ego. What does it mean, then?*

Response: "To die before you die" means to surrender completely. To surrender completely means ceasing to even recognize a phrase such as "identifying with the ego." To surrender is to know every particle of one's self, to know that this entirety is what we are, to accept completely that this entirety is totally incapable of being perfect, to offer this entirety to God despite its unworthiness, to be indifferent to death despite this knowledge of imperfection, and to accept whatever judgment God makes. To know and accept one's self is to have no recourse except to God's mercy. To offer this nothingness, we can only say, "I did my best." And the real responsibility upon us is only that.

Question: *Is it possible to will our self to engage in this potentially painful process of self-examination? If so, is this not another way of saying we must be courageous enough to attempt to storm the Gates of Paradise?*

Response: The real courage lies in dealing with the small issue of why we are annoyed or resentful or otherwise dragging our soul down when we experience the annoyance of the other failing us. In a microcosm, that small occurrence and that small expression of pettiness is a much larger lesson in knowing and transforming than any dramatic storming of any gates.

Chapter 10
On Virtues and Vices

FROM THE PERSPECTIVE OF THE PATH AND metaphysical doctrine, virtue is seen as part of our natural substance. This is because we are beings created by God and in His image. The flaws of the soul, the vices, are less real as they are layered on top of our natural substance by the conditions of existence and manifestation. Consequently, we must affirm the virtues—the highest of which are truth and Love—and not focus on the secondary qualities that existence has added to our souls. This is why we should not focus on a particular flaw or vice we may have, but instead work to practice the complementary virtue. This is an essential part of our path.

Reforming the World

The world swirls around us and shows us its beautiful side and its ugly side; it has always been thus. But we must not fall into its trap, the trap of seeing it as separate from our own souls. It is the greatest of errors to blame the world, as something outside of ourselves, for the errors and ugliness we see. What is the world if not a message from the Divine to us? Are we not supposed to see ourselves there? The accusation that the world is an error (or in error, if you prefer) only separates us from the classroom in which we are supposed to learn.

So far as I can tell, the world we live in is very much the same world as the one in which Cain slew Abel. The motives are the same, and the passions are the same. Certainly, the context and the instruments at hand are different, but that is not substantial. We, as individuals, must confront the same issues as the ones that confronted the contemporaries of Noah, Moses, Jesus, and Mohammad. The thought of reforming the world, of changing it for the better, without changing ourselves is an illusion.

We do not know how long the world will continue in its current path. But, however long that is, the vices and the virtues will continue to dance before us and ask us to choose sides. How long the dance will continue, no one knows. One day the sun will rise in the west and it will be over. But, in any event, it will certainly be over for us at some point; and none of us know if it will rise in the morning or if we will be here to see it. What is important for us is to think about this personally.

The State of Being

The basis on which you act has the most relevance to the soul. What you are calling "virtue" is external behavior, as though virtue is somehow related to political correctness. This is why many people think that if they merely volunteer to work in a soup kitchen, or take baskets of cookies to their neighbors, they are being virtuous. Dump out of your head the shadow of the Ancient Greeks as well as the idea that you can imitate virtue. Think in terms of a state of being, not a state of doing. As we go further, you will understand clearly that there is a state of existence in which we have shed that which veils the soul. It is a process of interrogation and elimination that steadily increases the clarity or, you might say, transparency of ourselves. Our acts then become a literal embodiment of this state.

Moses [24] is only responsible for himself. That is one of the truths in this story. Moses made the error of thinking himself better or superior when he judged the acts of the stranger, as

---

24. The story of Moses in the Quran (Surah Al-Kahf 18 verses 60–82) that is referred to here imparts the teaching that human knowledge can never comprehend God's ways or the reasons for various events that God allows to happen. In this particular revelation, the Prophet Moses is strongly advised not to criticize or question the seemingly inappropriate actions of the mysterious sage Al Khidr.

though he (Moses) was better in his judgments. Your acts are *not* "essentially out of your hands." They are very much in your hands. When you rid yourself of all sense of, and need for, confirmation of your superiority, you act without that thought. You act even while knowing that the consequences of your acts cannot be categorized as good in comparison to any other acts. They can only be characterized by your lack of thinking you are superior. This is humility.

Virtuous Acts

The ruthlessly honest knowing of yourself that makes room in you to know God requires recognition and elimination of veils such as dishonesty, hypocrisy, envy, and arrogance. The elimination of these (and other) veils then allows you to act as a constant embodiment of humility, gratitude, and awareness under all circumstances. This takes you out of conventional seeing and categorizing.

Back to Moses. He was outspoken in his criticisms of another's (apparently incomprehensible) actions. He would probably have done things differently in the same circumstances, but that would have been his decision and that decision would *de facto* have reflected his soul's state. If his subsequent act reflected *any* element of arrogance, envy, hatred, personal gain, or self-congratulation, these very states would increase within him and come to dominate his thoughts and his soul. Typically, he will deny this truth to himself.

But, if he makes his decision without those veils, he will know and accept that he surrenders the judgment of that act to God. He will not be trying to score points of any kind. However, the condition of his soul will be the highest of spiritual conditions because his act will only be according to the circumstances. It will not be an act done according to bad or good content, but the act required of one who has shed all the baggage of ego.

This does not mean that his acts are not forceful or purposeful. Sometimes virtue is mistakenly understood as some state of saintly behavior. Moses came down from Sinai with wrath, and acted to destroy the golden calf. People died. It was an act required by the circumstances, not by Moses wanting to demonstrate his power or impress himself. And this state opens the door that leads to Light.

Question: *I have read that one way to overcome vices is to try to replace them with the corresponding virtue. Is this a good practice?*

Response: You are correct in the principle of correcting a particular vice by trying to stress the corresponding virtue in your life. This is an important practice in dealing with vices and other fissures in the soul. The key to using this principle effectively is to not confuse the moral perspective with the metaphysical. We always have the right to affirm the good and may even be called into action to do so. But true as this may be, that perspective runs the risk of being individualistic and egotistical. The starting point is that in metaphysical understanding, the positive qualities (the virtues) are actually more real than the negative ones (the vices). From this perspective, virtue is understood not as a human quality but as a Divine attribute.

From a practical point of view—that of practice—we focus on the invocation of the Divine Name, which is pure, true, and absolute, not on the plane of moral contradictions and contingencies in which we find the world and our egos. Invocation is about God, not about us. In any event, at this point in your spiritual life, you should simply be practicing the invocation of the Name with concentration and regularity. This second element is of essential importance. Concentrate as best you can and make regular periods of invocation part of the fabric of your life. For the time being, this should constitute your interior practice, and you should leave for later specific or

TERRY MOORE

technical kinds of interior work.

Practically speaking, I know what it is like to be surrounded by my own flaws and shortcomings. It is necessary to observe these things and try to understand what they reveal about ourselves. Nevertheless, they are phenomena like others; understanding them and where they come from may be a help in negotiating the world and the path, but they are not the point. The point is to stand on and identify with the truth. This is what we do with and in God's Name. And so, the invocation is our true self and absolutely beyond vice or error. That is our true nature and substance; everything else is dust.

Question: *Should one expect a good outcome from good, virtuous intent?*

Response: The very phrase "virtuous intent" displays ego; the alternative could only be "malicious intent," and no ego will ever tell itself that its intent is malicious. Consequently, we do not work at being virtuous; we work at being objective. This is to act in accordance with the necessities of conditions. This really means to act without intent. In such acting, if the self is able to shed all interest in outcome, it can act according to the conditions present. By shedding the attachment to outcomes, the self eliminates even the thought that our act is going to be virtuous or that we *are* virtuous by reason of intent. Attachment to the outcome often results in excusing ourselves if the outcome is not good: "But my intent was good." But what does this say about us?

An extreme example would be that we can have little doubt that Hitler framed his intent as "good" when he conceived a plan to eliminate the Jews. Further, his ego would have equally considered its consequences to be "good" insofar as he succeeded. The conditions, however, did not necessitate this act. He conceived the conditions to rationalize his desire to manifest hatred.

126

And so, because his soul was crippled by hate, and he knew no way of seeing how spiritually useless hatred is, his acts themselves were framed and ruled by hatred, as was his "rational" analysis of what Germany required in order to be "pure."

The path of Self-knowledge would have led him to interrogate the nature of his capacity to hate and whether or not that capacity had qualities that led his *nafs*[25] to higher grounds of clarity regarding its usefulness.

Question: *Why do I break my promises so easily?*

Response: Let's say you aspire to be the Perfect Man. To do so, you understand, would require that you hold yourself to a standard of never breaking your word. When I say never, I mean never—the standard is that when you make a promise, there is *no* reason sufficient to break your promise. You would have to be careful when you made a promise not to make it lightly or casually, with the understanding that you really didn't have to keep it if you had a good enough reason to break it, and that you could always come up with a reason if you wanted to.

An absolute commitment to virtue, to any one of the Divine Names, cannot be parsed into relative terms. That is an intellectually flawed spiritual understanding of virtue itself. Virtue is an absolute. It means that you do not make such distinctions as: *If it is a big promise, I keep it; if it is a small promise, who cares?* The virtuous person does not make that distinction. The virtuous person holds himself or herself to an absolute standard that never wavers, and the virtuous person does not cheapen his or her word. Ever. And so if you understand the meaning of this small single line, and if you are getting closer, the two elements that you would be most likely to wrestle with are these: *Can I decide* (because this decision is yours to make) *that I will never*

---

25. *Nafs* (نَفْس) is an Arabic word occurring in the Quran, literally meaning "lower self," and has been translated as "psyche," "ego," or "soul."

break my word when I make a promise? And the second element is: *will I be able to meet that standard?* You will think you can't meet that standard. It's too tough, too absolute. The thing is, it isn't too tough; what it requires is disciplining your being, your lower self, your self, your mind—instead of taking the easy way out. But a person can do it. And the ways that you can do it are these: First you say: *I will never break my word.* Secondly, you have to pay attention. Every time you make a promise, you have to say: *If I give my word, I will never break it. My word alone will not be compromised. Ever.*

Now, in terms of spiritual growth and elevation, you are not in a position in which you have decided to embody a holy, Divine virtue. In terms of knowing yourself, the attention that is required to be discerning as to the value of your word and the refusal to give it cheaply cannot help but change your soul, because you would find it a struggle to do this very small thing. Don't promise to mail the letter. Say: "I will try to mail the letter tomorrow," and by saying that, you will not make a hypocrite of yourself. You will be honest. Or, if you say: "I'm forgetful; please remind me to mail the letter," you will also be honest and you will not compromise your virtue. The small things, done that way, which seem so small to you that you discount them, will not be easy, because you are used to excusing yourself. Your ego will continuously tell you: *It's okay. Here is another reason not to keep your promise.*

Every time that happens, you will have to say to yourself: *That's not a good enough answer. That's not a good enough reason for breaking my promise.* And that is the struggle. It is the flat statement to your own ego that you are never again going to make a promise that you are not going to keep. And you will say: *Oh, I could never meet that standard.* The reason you say that is because you think it is too tough a standard; you want it to be easy; you want your promise to mean nothing. But if your promise means nothing, you cannot then go before God and say, "You have to keep Your promises," because that statement is then absurd. You have done nothing to mirror God.

I emphasize: You *can* do it. You can say you will never break your word. Don't make any promises for a month. You'll see how often we all dole out meaningless promises routinely. This does not strengthen your soul. To make promises that have meaning, you have to discipline your soul. If you decide you can't do it, it weakens your soul.

Chapter 11
On Emotions

SOMETIMES SPIRITUAL TRAVELERS WILL ASK A question about how to deal with a particularly intense emotional state, whether it's love or anger or fear, and the response to that is usually to say, first of all, pay attention. Use your discernment to see it for what it is. And as you watch it, you will be able to see that it comes and it goes. And it will be replaced by another state that comes and goes. Maybe it will be familiar, or maybe it will be new; but if you watch, these things will come and go.

Now, you know that which is real does not come and go. God does not come and go. And it is in that discernment that so much of this knowledge is to be found. Yes, it's easier sometimes to see these in those peak moments of life, these moments of great faith or sorrow or love. But it's just as important—and I would say even more important—to be able to use discernment through the warp and woof of everyday life, because life is full of opportunities for this and that, for aversion and attraction.

The path is always present and immediate, and every moment we have the chance to make these observations, this discernment, and these choices. The path is present and immediate. But so is the goal of the path: realization, or liberation, is just as immediate as our own experience. We should accomplish the good and avoid that which is negative or contrary to it.

That sounds like an easy prescription for the spiritual life, and in many ways it is. But there's something much more subtle and much more powerful at work here. And that is that when you make a choice to do something positive or make a choice to avoid doing something that's negative or contrary, even if it is attractive to you—when you make that choice, at the same time you necessarily combat this false idea of a separate self.

You necessarily challenge that notion. As you continue to do this, this becomes clearer, and you finally defeat the idea of your being separate from God. This is, as I said, present and immediate, and is the substance of the path and is our obligation as spiritual travelers; and at the same time it is our liberation.

On Love

One of the problems with this topic is that there is love and there is Love. The issues involved in understanding these two are complicated greatly by the incessant use of the first combined with complete ignorance of the second. Further, both words are commonly perceived as referring to emotion: in the first case, a variable and fickle emotion, and in the second, an abstraction that is incomprehensible in terms of the actualities of corporeality. It is not a matter of what love "should" be (i.e., "shiningly unconditionally from the heart") but more a matter of what love/Love *is*—and *that* requires that we learn what it means to love, which in turn requires us to learn what the difference is between conditional and unconditional love.

This knowledge cannot be gained by mere declaration that we recognize the last two terms as being opposites, because they are not opposites. You cannot think that you can flip a switch and go from one to the other, much less think that you understand "unconditional" simply by defining the term. You can only know from having *experienced* this.

The issue is, how can I provide you with a way to go about this? This work is critically important, but it is exceedingly difficult, as it involves the hypersensitivity of the ego's desire to cling to a paradigm that is more or less a social convention. What I can ask you to do—which I leave entirely to your discretion, because it involves personal and esoteric (inner) contemplation that is objective without being either dishonest or judgmental —would be to reflect on a very close relationship with an "other" and address it in terms of conditions. To go close to the bone is to consider your relationship to your other half. What conditions qualify the love you have for your spouse? How does your spouse fail to meet your needs? You do not have to answer these questions to me, but, if you take this challenge, you'll have to answer them to yourself. I'll be interested to know what you learn about love and about yourself.

Question: *How should I deal with anxiety over the future of my children?*

Response: We are responsible for our children, and we must do the best we can; but we must remember that, before they are our children, they are God's creatures with their own destinies, which we cannot determine. Therefore, it is necessary for us to recognize that we can only have a certain amount of influence over the lives of our children and that we must leave the rest in the Hands of God.

This does not mean, of course, that we cannot plan for our children's future, or do all that we can do to provide for them in all ways. But we must do so with great humility toward God, in recognition of the fact that these things are, ultimately, not in our hands. Without doubt, the very best thing we can do for our children is to be good people—this will stand as a testament and a treasure beyond all other gifts. They will get incomparably more from us by knowing who we are than they will get by simply knowing what we think or say about things.

It is usual to want our children to have successful lives in every way. But we should also keep in mind that—as with all human situations—we do not know the future. Often our children's lives do not work out as we intend, yet we must never despair; God may have plans for our children that we cannot foresee. The future belongs to Him.

Question: *Why do I feel so much pain and suffering? I feel as though we need to expose ourselves to a certain kind of pain and suffering.*

Response: You have chosen one route to the exclusion of the entirety. Why do you not equally speak of exposing your ego and body to considerable experiences of joy, peace, love, and happiness? These too can serve to wrench you from your ego, when you recognize the nanoseconds of intellection that occur more often than you believe and give you a taste of the light of the Self. You can choose to let your wonderful mind experience more of those wonderful nanoseconds by dropping the various useless parts of your ingrained habits and certainties.

The fact that you see this project as an heroic struggle keeps you in the cold and reinforces the notion that you are worthless and far removed from God. God has given you all the tools you need. Who causes the pain and suffering that you say we need to expose our egos and bodies to? You do not make the decisions to expose yourself to pain and suffering. God makes those decisions. And He make the decisions about both the good things that happen to you and the trials. So when you say: *We need to expose ourselves....* who is speaking here? It is as though you chose the amount of pain and suffering. Do you similarly choose the number of good things?

Question: *How do you react to evil in the world without getting angry, especially when you know that you are right?*

Response: I can give you answers, but I'm not going to. You are angry because the world does not function as you wish it to. You are frantic and outraged because you cannot stop it from being what it is. If you were given the power to dictate the world's behavior, you believe it would be better. This is the same as saying you believe you know better than God. In truth, the world is perfect for its intended purpose. It cannot be otherwise.

When you can tell me why it is perfect for its intended purpose, you will no longer need anyone's advice. At the moment, you want quick, glib aphorisms that solve this problem. You want the punchline first. I will not give it to you. It seems that it is not only in California that you can find places that purport to peddle "Ten Steps to Enlightenment." Not here. Keep reading. Look more deeply into yourself. Look more deeply into the world.

Nothing will prevent you from acting, nor from acting to prevent injustice to others. You are beginning to see that your acts can occur while you remain free of the trap of thinking that the world is not perfect. The world is perfect for its intended purpose. It is demonstrating that very truth within you right now. You are changing, rising to a higher level of understanding—one that does not require either indifference toward or rejection of the world. The world exists solely to allow individual souls to know God through knowing themselves.

Such knowledge is not accomplished by gathering information, but by the far deeper task of recognizing meaning. When you know that if you were God you would have created the world exactly the same way He did, you will know it is purposeful in every respect. Few reach this knowledge. You have the capacity to do so.

It is vital to your spiritual progress that you surrender hate, because hate makes you, by definition, one whose soul is blocked from truth. Humanity is a bell curve. Long before modern governments existed, kings, princes, and tribal chieftains pillaged and looted to acquire power and riches. Every sacred Scripture since time began has recognized this. The fact that many will never attain to either understanding of truth or transformation of themselves is a fact. To allow this fact to cause you to exist in an imprisoned state is a logical absurdity, an emotional absurdity, and a spiritual absurdity.

It is not necessary to disengage from the world. On the contrary, to follow esotericism, you must instead go to the core of it and of you. To answer your question: Yes, I am encouraging you to see yourself in the world in order to elevate your soul through self-knowledge—self-knowledge of a certain kind in a certain way, which is the esoteric path, the path of personal interior knowledge.

When you can understand that the human condition does not need to cause you to respond with anger or hate, and when you understand that creation is a perfect classroom for the individual soul, and when you have undertaken the work of changing your state, your perceptions will change. You will feel pity for those who have condemned themselves to the spiritual misery of thinking that acquisition will somehow make them immortal or god-like. Such people spend the last moments of life in a state of terror. If you want to be superior to them, then feel pity for them, for that is what compassion really means, and it is precisely why we are here.

But we can only know this truth after our own state of existence has been changed. If others choose not to aspire to truth, all the more reason for your pity. God willing, you may one day know (as a state of existence) that the world is perfect for its intended purpose, because the world will have participated in the transformation of you.

We have all encountered hypocrisy and evil. We need not respond with hate. We must choose a higher state by becoming a higher state of spiritual existence. Many saints and prophets have railed against man's failure to abide by God's commands. Though their words were harsh, they were not driven by hate, but by compassion. You want me to engage in an intellectual/philosophical dialectic with you, but it is you that is the issue. You do not have to cling to your former idols. They have no power over you except the power you give them. Your view does not have to be based on anger or hate, even when you act to avoid evil or protect someone else from it. Nor does your view need to be based on a gushy New Age conception of love.

These are mistaken stereotypes.

To stop loving a person or institution or society as a whole because it lacks perfection or virtue is spiritually useless, and is also a misuse of the word "love." To know and accept all allows you to see yourself in all. It does not force you to hate it or adopt the person's, institution's, or society's ways; instead, it should contribute to your own humility. To see from this higher level of objectivity is to choose to take a higher spiritual step. And there, and with even more knowledge, we drop hate and learn to pray for others, rather than excoriating them, that they might open their eyes and see that there is another way, a way that leads to certainty and transcendence.

As for love, to love does not mean to love indiscriminately. Compassion, however, is divinely indiscriminate. To write or speak from the soul's compassion is to be informed by truth and, in a certain sense, hope. These are states that reflect the very essence of God. They are not weaknesses.

You speak about being right. Concerning rightness, many who celebrate how right they are come to the end of life in a state of bitterness and resentment because their rightness is all that they have. They are angry that those in the wrong did not fall to their knees in acknowledgment and defeat. If you think about this, who would choose such a state? Perhaps such people expect a trophy of some kind, listing all the times they were right and others were wrong. Cold comfort indeed.

The issue is not your rightness; it is the state of your soul. The truth of the world as you articulate it is not the same as knowing truth. And, as you rightly perceive, you are stuck in the defensive position of demanding proof that you are wrong in your assessments of the world. Such proofs are the ransom that must be paid in order for you to believe. You say that we all put forth our opinions of what we think the truth is, including me. The difference is that the truth I speak of, the truth that lies beneath and throughout creation, can raise our state of existence to levels of awareness and perception and ascension that obliterate the illusions of corporeality and make it blindingly clear that the One is the Real.

I don't think so. I am so. Belief is not the pinnacle. "Belief" is not a synonym for "knowing." Fervent belief leads just as easily to violence as to naïveté. Knowing truth is a state of existence in which all things are theophany. Perhaps you imagine me sitting upon a lotus pad all day being "spiritual," but I assure you I am not naïve; I am well acquainted with the ways of the world. It is perfect for its intended purpose.

Interrogate the usefulness of your anger and alienation. Draw these two creatures close to your bosom and ask them how on earth they have managed to dominate your state of being. Examine whether any of the effects they have help you feel happier, more peaceful, more able to behold a leaf with awe. See that these creatures are not the gigantic, powerful beasts you think they are. They are gremlins. Refuse to exist in that state. You are more powerful than they, and you can teach them to stand aside. Keep looking for the higher. The proofs are all around you.

Question: *How should one mentally and emotionally handle the various atrocities that go on in the world each day?*

Response: You ask about how to respond emotionally to the atrocities you hear about on the news. It is best to understand questions like this on the basis of first principles. There is a principle that to every action there is a reaction: This is so on every level of reality, from the spiritual world to everyday life (of course, this is not to dispense with God's Mercy, or exceptions that occur through the Divine Will). What the Hindus call the law of karma is an application of that universal principle to everyday life. Every action entails a reaction. The spiritual traveler should always try to see evil in the world in terms of this larger picture, and not in a small frame, which can distort events so that they even seem to contradict God's Mercy and His Justice. We must avoid these truncated interpretations that substitute the part for the whole. To make this kind of substitution is very dangerous, both spiritually and intellectually.

So we should always have compassion, but partial compassion is a very dangerous thing. It's a form of hypocrisy, which we spiritual travelers must always avoid. Of course, you're sadder if your cat dies than if some cat dies in Burma; that's natural. But we should strive to have compassion for the whole of creation, and not concentrate all our emotional energy on one instance of a heinous crime. We must bring objectivity to our own emotional reactions. It is important to situate individual instances of crime and suffering within global circumstances.

It is easy to relate to your question as I, too, am disturbed by violence imposed on any innocent, and particularly upon animals. Of course, it would be easy to tell you to not read the news or watch television. There is a certain amount of wisdom in that approach, as we must all weigh and manage the things in our lives that distract and distress us. We must always look to all of our experience for clues and indications that help us along in our spiritual work. This means that it does not matter whether or not you watch the news; but what does matter, and is of critical spiritual importance, is that you understand your experience. You must understand that everything in the world—including the news and how you experience it—exists solely for the purpose of helping you to know yourself and—through that—to know God. Otherwise, you and your experience would not be here at all.

Your question is very important, because it touches upon the purpose of the world: not its purpose in itself, but its purpose for you. The first thing you have to understand is that the world exists so that you might know yourself, and thereby know

God. The world is a classroom, and it is perfect for its intended purpose. There is nothing in the world—not even the horrors that upset you so much—that cannot expand your awareness of yourself and lead you to greater knowledge of God. That is its purpose, and yours.

It is said that the microcosm reflects the macrocosm. The application here is in recognizing that the things you see in the world around you—however disturbing they may be—also exist in your own soul. Otherwise, how would you be able to recognize them? So you must find where these things exist in your own soul. You must be ruthlessly honest and objective to know yourself. Take the word "objective" absolutely literally. The fundamental purpose of corporeality is to allow you to see yourself. This cannot be done prior to manifestation into the corporeal realm because, prior to manifestation, your existence is nothing more than a possibility within God where your only awareness is awareness of God. You do not have, nor can you have, self-awareness, until you arrive in a realm whose conditions include the illusion of subject and object. In manifestation, we also find God as well as things that are not God, and so there will be fractures and flaws in existence; these are the things we know as "evil."

Corporeality presents itself as an unending panorama of phenomena. It is a deliberate and purposeful creation. You bounce off corporeality every minute, which reflects back, like a mirror, the condition and state of your soul. Only under conditions of polarity and duality (i.e., contrast) can you see yourself, and only by seeing your soul's actual composition and condition can you learn (or not) to actually know yourself. Every thought, every act, every response you have to the world is a reflection of your soul's state. This is usually clearer during moments of great danger, or crisis, or in your exposure to situations to which you have a strong emotional response. For all of these situations you should give thanks, then try to learn the lesson.

To know yourself without pseudo-psychological judgment—to know the totality—is necessary to knowing God. This exploration will reveal to you many facets and states of your own soul. Once you see them objectively, you will be able to put them in their proper place. You will be able to spend more time with the ones that are higher and closer to God. You will also be able to discern which of these aspects and qualities are useless, waste your time, and take you away from things that are higher. When you identify which of those things are useless, you can shed them. To shed what is useless is to open the Eye of the Heart. To open the Eye of the Heart is to let Light replace darkness. All veils disappear. To exist in Light is God's wish for your soul.

For example, when you first hear about one of these traumatic news stories, pay attention: What is your first thought? That thought, whatever it was, had nothing whatsoever to do with the news story. It had to do with what you are. If your first thought was: *I'm so glad I wasn't there*, this will tell you something true about yourself. If your first thought was: *Why doesn't somebody do something about this?*, that, too, reveals yourself to yourself. Most people cannot bear to know themselves in a way that leads to spiritual growth. Their egos only accept input that flatters. They blame God, they blame "bad people," they blame the world. They miss the point that the world is perfect for its intended purpose—and that this purpose is so that you can know God.

All of this is very stark, and instead of offering you a way to be protected from the anguish you feel, I am telling you to embrace it as a spiritual benefit. But that is not the whole story. Our only escape from this anguish is through God and with His help. The greatest help He has given us is His Name, which is more real than any of the phenomena around you and leads directly to knowledge of Him. Think of the invocation as kind of life raft that God has given you personally. Hold to it as a still point amid the flux and chaos of life. It is always within reach. It is always the right answer.

When the world is too much with us [26] (as when you are upset or worried about the things you hear on the news and elsewhere), it is necessary to seek refuge in our hearts, in the interior life, and we long for an opportunity to step out of the world—to take a spiritual retreat—and concentrate on what's important. Yet on the other hand, we must live in the world. This is a question of balance that we must all work out ourselves. The sacred rites provide a great protection and a great strength. So does the path in the instruction and support it offers us. It is our duty to invoke God in our hearts and learn from this perfect classroom in which He has placed us so that we can learn about ourselves, so that we might come to know Him.

---

26. *The World Is Too Much With Us* by William Wordsworth, C.1802 CE

Chapter 12
On Religion and the Direct Path[27]

Introduction

WHEN I FOUND THE DIRECT PATH,[28] I WASN'T looking for a path; I already had a path, and a good one. For more than 40 years I have been a Perennialist and a member of a Sufi order, or *tariqah*. So why would I look for anything more?

Over the last several years, I had begun to feel that that my own practices had become too abstract and conceptualized, and in many ways rote and dry. My discovery of the direct path refocused my practices and helped me discover elements that were lacking in my particular use and experience of them. These were methodological keys that were not missing from Sufism, but that had never been clear or actualized in my own practice.

These keys and the perspective from which they came have clarified and filled in much of the methodology of my Sufi practice. My commitment to Sufism has been rekindled and strengthened, and I have learned new ways of understanding the prayers, invocation, and rituals that I have been doing for years. The direct-path approach has given them light and life and returned to me the wonder, joy, and enthusiasm for the sake of which I entered Sufism in the first place.

This ability of the direct path to enliven and illuminate the practice of Sufism surely extends to the practice of religion in general. In fact, the direct path and religion enhance each other: the direct path breathes life into the practice of religion,

27. This essay originally appeared in *Real-World Nonduality: Reports from the Field*, ed. Greg Goode (2019), and is reprinted here with the kind permission of the publisher, New Sarum Press.
28. The direct path is a nondual teaching of self-realization, inspired by Sri Atmananda (Krishna Menon).

and the practice of religion prepares the heart for the direct path by clearing the road to the Absolute.

Perennialism and Religion

This harmony between religion and the direct path is best understood from my own perspective not only as a Sufi, but also as a Perennialist. Perennialism goes by many names: Perennial Philosophy, Perennial Religion, *Sophia Perennis*, Traditionalism, and others. The root of the Perennialist perspective is the view that all of the world's religious traditions share a single, universal, and transcendent source and foundation. Perennialism is not a practice, but a lens through which the manifold religious and spiritual doctrines and practices of the world become intelligible according to their metaphysical source and means of transcending the personal in light of the Universal. This understanding is expressed in the title of Perennialist author Frithjof Schuon's famous book *The Transcendent Unity of Religions*.[29]

The Importance of Orthodoxy in Practice

My own journey brought me to Perennialism before it brought me to Sufism. But, as I said above, Perennialism is not a practice, not a religion. Fortunately, the Perennialist authors I had discovered were very clear on the need for not only religious practice, but practice within an orthodox framework. I knew most of the Perennialists I had been reading were attached to a Sufi *tariqah* that was not only Perennialist in its orientation but also orthodox in its practices.

This question of orthodoxy was, for me, extremely important in considering the choice of a spiritual path. I was seeking a path that, in the words of Frithjof Schuon, "participate[s], by

29. Frithjof Schuon, 1984: *The Transcendent Unity of Religions*, Quest Books, Wheaton, Illinois.

way of a doctrine that can properly be called 'traditional,' in the immutability of the principles which govern the Universe and fashion our intelligence."[30] Although orthodoxy does not guarantee enlightenment, it is an extremely powerful means of protecting oneself from error. It was a great comfort to me to know that the path I was choosing had a long and honorable history and that it was not one person's idea or a newcomer on the scene.

Much of my feeling about the importance of orthodoxy comes from personal experience and contact with people who have had powerful mystical experiences. What is often problematic about these experiences is that those who have them have no greater context in which to situate what has happened to them. As a result, they end up making it up by themselves and trying to formulate from scratch a doctrine and method that can explain and recapitulate their own experience.

One cautionary tale of the hazards of mysticism without orthodoxy comes from my personal experience with someone I will call "Mr. Rose." Mr. Rose was a farmer from rural Ohio who had been overwhelmed by a powerful mystical experience one day on his tractor while planting soybeans. He struck me as an intelligent and sincere man, and he spoke with considerable conviction and charisma. By the time I went to meet him, he had collected a small clutch of young people around him who were pursuing the experience that he described with such great conviction. In addition to attending meetings at which he would discuss his views, everyone in the group would spend so many hours a week driving a tractor, as Mr. Rose had been doing when he was overtaken by the experience. Tractor-driving was new to me as a mystical method.

Unfortunately, this story is rather typical in the history of mysticism. One can think of examples from classical and

30. *Christianity/Islam: Essays on Esoteric Ecumenicism.* Trans. Gustavo Polit. Bloomington, Ind.: World Wisdom Books, 1985

medieval times, yet there are examples even in the present day. In the 1960s, the band The Who produced the rock opera *Tommy*, which tells the story of just such a person and experience: a deaf, dumb, and blind boy who had a flash of enlightenment while playing pinball. Many acknowledged his "miracle" and sought to learn from him. He instructed them in the method that had worked for him, by giving his disciples eyeshades and earplugs and leading them to a pinball machine. But they were unable to have the same experience for themselves, and they ended up rejecting Tommy and his teaching. History is full of such stories; rarely is the music so good.

In the search for an authentic path, one often finds people like Mr. Rose, people who have had a powerful experience and now say they can teach you to transcend your own blindness and limitations so that you, too, can experience Reality/Illumination/Enlightenment/the Beatific Vision. But can they? How could you know? The problem is that even if Mr. Rose's experience is genuine, he cannot situate it in terms of a doctrine and method that is complete enough to be helpful to others. He has no comprehensive context in which to express who he is and what the world is, so he cannot convey the real breadth and depth of his experience. It is all too common for someone to have an individualized and fragmentary experience that he takes for full enlightenment, and it is a considerable limitation to his teaching if he has no access to the doctrinal and methodological resources that would make it easier to communicate to others.

This is a powerful argument for traditional orthodoxy. Sufism has had 1,500 years to work out and perfect its spiritual methodology. Buddhists claim 2,500 years of helping people to transcend themselves. Finding a master of any kind is a serious undertaking, and the seeker needs to be as sure as possible of the master's credentials. Tradition and orthodoxy do not guarantee enlightenment, but they do greatly decrease the risk for the seeker of wasting his or her time or even life.

Religion has a long and proven history of bringing transcend-ent peace to countless millions and providing us with thousands of years of enlightened and realized sages and saints, most of whom made their journey to enlightenment in the context of religious practice. I suspect that virtually all of those great lights would assert that their religious practice was essential to their journey to liberation and realization.

What Can Religion Do for the Direct Path?

One of the remarkable things about the direct path is that its doctrine is so clear: Awareness is everything, and all other things—objects, thoughts, feelings—are really just arisings in awareness. Period.

But how does the traveler absorb this simple truth? As all mystical travelers find out sooner or later, there is a difference between understanding a truth and realizing the truth in its full depth. A theoretical understanding of reality is insufficient; we must live the understanding and make it part of our own experience.

A conceptual understanding of reality is certainly necessary, and it can prompt and encourage the practice through which it becomes real knowledge. But relying only on conceptual know-ledge can inhibit and truncate one's journey by substituting mere answers for the experiential response that questions need. Worst of all, a conceptual understanding can become simply a locus of identity and affiliation that gives travelers a sense of belonging to a kind of elite philosophy club that grants them an exalted status high and above the benighted souls who don't know the doctrine or speak its code words.

Conceptual knowledge may be a beginning, but the point is to make our knowing our being. It is precisely in this pro-ject that religion offers its assistance to the direct path. Every traditional and orthodox form contains doctrines and practices that facilitate the very objective the direct path offers so succinctly. Further, traditional religion gives the direct path a practice and environment in which to operate, highly useful tools, and a practical discipline that nurtures direct-path inquiry. In conjunction, tradition and the direct path form a kind of organic whole in which to live life and practice the path to awareness, liberation, enlightenment—whatever you want to call it.

Let me offer you an example from my own practice of Sufism of how religion can bring the truth offered by the direct path out of the realm of mere conceptual knowledge and into the life of the traveler. At the heart of Sufi practice is the *dhikr Allah*, the invocation of the great Name of God, Allah (literally "The God."). This kind of invocation is the same spiritual form of practice one finds throughout the world of mystical spirituality. Other traditions know it by other names. It is the "prayer of the heart" of Christianity, the *nembutsu* of Buddhism, the *japa* of Hinduism. It is the technique of focusing the mind on a single sound or image and its repetition, which frees the mind from its constant circling and seeking of distraction. The very nature of the Name-sound-image, combined with the earnestness and intention of the practitioner, provides the power to liberate the separate self from its illusion of separate existence. The practice takes the doctrine of the direct path—that the separate existence of the self is an illusion—and allows it to be realized in the heart of the person who is invoking the Name.

In addition, the areas of practical life—especially matters of virtue and morality—are well covered by the great religious traditions, which now in the light of the direct path offer a comprehensive view of life while we are on the path of return to the source. It may be easy to see how compatible direct-path practice is with religion and traditional forms of spirituality, but it can be less clear how the direct path alone addresses the daily and practical issues that the religions deal with so specifically. Traditions offer a secure framework in which to make these decisions.

Another advantage of practicing a traditional form of religion—and this one is of particular importance for those who practice the direct path—is that traditional religion is a hedge against nihilism. It is all too easy to read some nondualist teachings that emphasize the point that personal agency does not exist, and conclude that there is no doer, no doing, and—consequently and necessarily—nothing to be done. This is one of those things that is true in principle but not in practice. By contrast, the direct path is all about practice, beginning and most fundamentally with the practice of doing self-inquiry. We all have to do. Our days are full of doing things. It cannot be otherwise. That being true, the question arises: what *should I do? What is the* right thing *to do? Or, more fully presented: what* decisions *can I make? What* practices *can I take up that will facilitate my learning and knowing so that my theoretical knowledge of the truth of existence will become my experience and my lived reality?* We are constantly presented with experiences that suggest we have a choice. We should intend the right thing and act accordingly. We should always choose that which makes the real more real, and the less real less real. We choose, and then we experience the result.

It is in this realm that traditional religion has much to offer the seeker in conjunction with the direct path. Religion and tradition are derived from the Ultimate Good and provide a context for living life and making the quotidian decisions of life easier by supplying a context and an attitude that conforms the seeker to the journey that he or she is taking. Religion and tradition supply points of reference for moral decision-making, which often relieves the stress of having so many things to decide. Further, they require a commitment on the part of the seeker, which weakens the false separate self by submitting it to that which is higher, more real, more true. They subordinate personal desire to divine Reality. They also prescribe for us attitudes for our understanding and our conduct, which are of critical importance for our journey. Our attitudes, according to the twentieth-century nondualist guru Nisargadatta,[31] are one of the few things we have any control over. Obviously, we should conform our attitudes to that which is most facilitative of our knowing the real.

What Can the Direct Path Do for Religion?

I am a Sufi. Sufism is often defined as "Islamic mysticism." This is accurate, as it situates Sufism within the body of an orthodox tradition with all its formal practices, sacred history, religious and mystical scholarship, and wisdom traditions passed down through the generations. But after years of practice, I found that my own use of the method offered by my *tariqah* had become mechanical and ineffective. I was faithful to the practice, but could not deny the feeling that my spiritual life had ceased to grow, that it was stalled and stale.

It was my discovery of the direct path that brought into my own practice the essential notion of examining my own experience. To my great surprise, there were many dimensions of the experience of invocation that I had never focused on or examined. The introduction of the notions of experience and inquiry have made every second of my practice rich and spiritually efficacious. Similarly, these direct-path concepts and methods have shed light on and given life to myriad spiritual and religious practices that previously seemed obscure or even silly to me.

For example, one of the themes of meditation used in the invocation of the Divine Name is the concept of transcendence—that God is perfect in His absoluteness, beside which

31. Nisargadatta, 2012 *I am That*, The Acorn Press, Durham, NC.

we are nothing. This no longer seems like a philosophical or metaphysical axiom to this traveler, but a stage in the process of knowing the real. The point here is that we must first find out what we are not in order to find out what we really are.

The introduction of direct-path methods of inquiry has also added an element of interior spiritual guidance that had not been part of the milieu in which I learned this method. This lack was clearly a shortcoming. The direct path, with its emphasis on inquiry and the examination of experience, pointed the way for me to ask the questions that would make my own path live again.

There is a wonderful complementarity and harmony between Sufism and the direct path. With its emphasis on the primacy of experience, the direct path opens the meaning of what Sufism calls "tasting." Tasting is necessarily experiential and direct. This was the discovery that laid bare for me the value of the interrogation of personal experience. For example, one major change in my own practice has to do with presence. In Sufism, I have always understood the importance of being fully present in all the rites and activities. In order for the practices to be efficacious, one must be fully present. God demands all that we are, not simply our bodies or our minds reciting rote formulations. This kind of presence had always played an important role in my own practice. But now I see the rites and practices not as an occasion to make myself present, but as an occasion to remove my self and taste what is actually present. The effort is not to place myself into the practice but to get my self out of the way by focusing on the presence of the Real.

This has become my focus when I am in meditation, invocation, and sacred dance. Much language has been given to the notion of practicing the presence of God. But now it seems this way: the awareness of the presence of God is in fact the presence of the awareness of God. This discovery from the direct path has been essential in transforming my own practice from being about performance to being about awareness. And so the focus of my spiritual life has become more about the use of my attention and awareness than about performance. It has become more about being than about doing.

There is a great deal of literature and doctrine about the nature of the soul and its problems. Sufism provides complex descriptions of the different levels of the soul and its operation. Prior to my discovery of the direct path, many of these carefully worked-out explanations seemed like doctrine, that is, something to be learned and, perhaps, observed. But for the spiritual traveler, it is not enough to know the various aspects of the soul only in principle; they have to be experienced. The traveler needs to see them, along with the limitations of each, in action.

In this way the direct path showed me that doctrine is not an end in itself. But this new understanding of the place of experience in the spiritual life is not simply an intellectual "Aha!" for me; it changes the very substance of the spiritual path—or, at least, it does for me. It has taken all the dead and brittle facts and doctrinal principles I was already well acquainted with and breathed life into them. The wisdom of the sages is no longer something to be appreciated and learned and understood, but rather something to be lived here and now.

For example, one of the doctrines found throughout Islam and Sufism is a description of the soul, usually the "lower soul"[32] with its various problems, opacities, passions, and errors. The Arabic term used for the soul is *nafs* (similar to the Hebrew *nephesh*, "animal spirit"). This is generally what the direct path and similar teachings refer to as the mind-body. This is the plane of battle for the greater holy war (*jihad al-akbar*). Sufism, similarly to other spiritual paths, can be described as a struggle with one's soul or a *jihad* with the *nafs*. I always thought I had

32. "Lower soul" refers to the constellation of impressions, feelings, ideas and memories that are usually mistaken for "myself." This is the territory of the mind, which can only know ideas. It acts in its own interest on its own level and would rather defend its separateness than sacrifice itself.

understood this concept, and I took it in the context of this same battle from St. Paul: "I do not understand what I do. For what I want to do I do not do, but what I hate I do" (Romans 7:15).

Finally, thanks to the direct path, I understood that the effort (*jihad*) here is not to defeat the qualities of the soul. Defeating them would mean engaging them, which would give them more reality than they actually have. The effort is not to defeat the qualities of the soul, but rather to penetrate the illusion that they exist at all.

In providing instructions for carrying out this process, the direct path opened for me a key insight into the fundamental doctrine of my own religion. In Islam, the greatest sin is *shirk*, attributing partners to God. The fundamental principle of Islam is that there is only one God, and that He is "not begotten, not begetting, and that there is none comparable to Him" (Quran 112). So, if this is true, then who is this *nafs* that I must struggle against?

The direct path cleared this doubt about the *nafs* in a practical and useful way. This battle with the soul was not to engage it and tame it; rather the battle was to examine its qualities and behavior and determine what, if anything, it really was. Previously I had been all too willing to blithely go along in my spiritual practice and think that maybe someday I would come to know God. But this is a principal error that introduces dualism into a religion that is fundamentally an expression of Divine Unity. There isn't any "me and God"; there is only God.

The teaching about the *nafs* is just one example of the doctrines that are expressed in dualistic terms but can be—and must be—resolved to the One. For those who accept the basic doctrine of the faith, finally, there is no other conclusion possible.

Another key that the direct path has to offer traditional religions has to do with how to understand the place of religious experiences. Traditional religious practice tends to be dismissive of experiences, and understandably so, particularly for us children of the psychedelic era. The goal is to have a spiritual life, not a series of spiritual experiences. Tradition discourages centering the spiritual life around experiences, because the spiritual life is not about entertaining oneself, regardless of how lofty these experiences may be. The direct path opened my eyes to the proper place of experience in a clear and dramatic way, first by showing me clearly that tradition is right: experiences are beside the point; but at the same time—and this was what was so dramatic—experience, as such, is the point. The roadblock is the gate. As Ibn 'Arabi says, the things that veil us from God are the very things He uses to reveal Himself to us. Experiences are irrelevant, but experience, as such, is the key.

The direct path takes experience as a starting point and calls into question what we previously accepted as knowledge, insisting that only the evidence provided by direct experience is reliable. At the same time, it gives the seeker full responsibility and assumes his competence—under the guidance of his teacher—to perform the discernment required to verify the truth of the teachings. The direct path's process is to perform the experiment to "see for yourself" rather than simply to believe. The only fundamental belief, which must at least be present as an intuition, is the sole reality of the One. The direct path thus gives the seeker tools for bringing what begins as a detached, merely intellectual belief into his or her immediate experience. These direct-path keys that have so enriched my practice of Sufism are available to other traditional religions as well.

Harmony between Religion and the Direct Path

Religion is more than just a finger pointing at the moon. Each authentic tradition speaks to the whole of the person, to the spirit and the soul and the body, and by bringing all of these levels of the microcosm into play—by providing doctrine for the mind, moral precepts for the will, objects of devotion for the sentiment, and ritual for the body—it serves to protect us against the hypertrophy or deviation of any one of these levels. Seen through the direct-path lens, all of these things become operative tools for learning and growing. In this way, religion enhances the direct path, and the direct path enhances religion.

For these reasons, it is clear that there is a great possibility for synthesis and harmony between the direct path and the practice of traditional religion. I have experienced this harmony in my own practice. More than once, I have heard experienced direct-path teachers comment that students from a structured background seem to do better in the direct path than those from non-believing or non-practicing backgrounds. We certainly come here as we are. But once we have arrived here, it would seem that a strong traditional practice in light of and in conjunction with the direct path provides the most efficacious choice for life and path.

Similarly, I have known several men and women who adhere strongly to their traditional faith and have discovered the direct path. None have considered leaving their tradition. All have given thanks to God for the advent in their lives of direct-path teaching. Traditional practice, with its insistence on goodness, honor, compassion, generosity, and the other virtues, provides a kind of holistic Royal Road to the Absolute.

For Further Reading

(Alphabetically by title)

Perennialism

Ancient Beliefs and Modern Superstitions, Martin Lings

The Book of the Way and Its Virtue, Lao Tzu (Tao Te Ching)

The Crisis of the Modern World, René Guénon

The Essential Writings of Frithjof Schuon, ed. Seyyed Hossein Nasr

Ideals and Realities of Islam, Seyyed Hossein Nasr

Light on the Ancient Worlds, Frithjof Schuon

Religion and the Order of Nature, Seyyed Hossein Nasr

The Spiritual Ascent (Treasury of Traditional Wisdom), ed. Whitall Perry

The Tao of Islam, Sachiko Murata

The Transcendent Unity of Religions, Frithjof Schuon

The Way of a Pilgrim, poss. Archimandrite Mikhail Kozlov (1826–1884) and Arsenii Troepolskii (1804–1870)

Understanding Islam, Frithjof Schuon

Zen and the Art of Archery, Eugen Herrigel

Sufism

Esoterism as Principle and as Way, Frithjof Schuon

The Garden of Truth, Seyyed Hossein Nasr

Ibn Arabi's works (various translations)

Introduction to Sufi Doctrine, Titus Burckhardt

Knowledge and the Sacred, Seyyed Hossein Nasr

Stations of Wisdom, Frithjof Schuon

A Sufi Saint of the Twentieth Century, Martin Lings

What is Sufism?, Martin Lings

Art

Sacred Art in East and West, Titus Burckhardt

Shakespeare in the Light of Sacred Art, Martin Lings

Nondualism

Book of Certainty, Martin Lings

I Am, Jean Klein

Standing as Awareness, Greg Goode

The Transparency of Things, Rupert Spira

Who Am I?, Jean Klein

CONVERSATIONS ON AWAKENING
Interviews by Iain and Renate McNay

Conversations on Awakening features 24 unique accounts of Awakening all taken from transcripts of interviews made for conscious.tv.

Some of the interviewees are renowned spiritual teachers while others are completely unknown having never spoken in public or written a book.

These conversations will hopefully encourage you, inspire you, and maybe even guide you to find out who you really are.

Conversations on Awakening: Part One features interviews with A.H Almaas, Jessica Britt, Sheikh Burhanuddin, Linda Clair, John Butler, Billy Doyle, Georgi Y. Johnson, Cynthia Bourgeault, Gabor Harsanyi, Tess Hughes, Philip Jacobs and Igor Kufayev.

Conversations on Awakening: Part Two features interviews with Susanne Marie, Debra Wilkinson, Richard Moss, Mukti, Miek Pot, Reggie Ray, Aloka (David Smith), Deborah Westmorland, Russel Williams, Jurgen Ziewe, Martyn Wilson and Jah Wobble.

Published by White Crow Books.
Available from Amazon in ebook and paperback format and to order from all good bookstores.
Part one: p.282, ISBN: 978-1786770936
Part two: p.286, ISBN: 978-1786770950

www.conscious.tv

Books in print from New Sarum Press

Real World Nonduality—Reports From The Field; Various authors

The Ten Thousand Things by Robert Saltzman

Depending on No-Thing by Robert Saltzman

The Joy of True Meditation by Jeff Foster

'What the...' A Conversation About Living by Darryl Bailey

The Freedom to Love—The Life and Vision of Catherine Harding by Karin Visser

Death: The End of Self-Improvement by Joan Tollifson

2020 Publications

Glorious Alchemy—Living the Lalita Sahasranama by Kavitha Chinnaiyan

Collision with the Infinite by Suzanne Segal

Transmission of the Flame by Jean Klein

The Ease of Being by Jean Klein

Open to the Unknown by Jean Klein

Yoga in The Kashmir Tradition (2nd Edition) by Billy Doyle

The Mirage of Separation by Billy Doyle

Looking Through God's Eyes by Han van den Boogaard

The Genesis of Now by Rich Doyle

Fly Free by Dami Roelse

Advaitaholics Anonymous by Shiv Sengupta

www.newsarumpress.com

Made in the USA
Middletown, DE
10 March 2021

35200387R00104